WILL YOU NOT REASON?

WILL YOU NOT REASON?

God's arguments in the Qur'an

SAID MIRZA

Men of God
Publishing

Third Edition, 2023

ISBN 978-1-7336408-5-5

The Qur'an: A Complete Revelation © Sam Gerrans, 2021.
The Meaning of the Holy Qur'an © Abdullah Yusuf Ali, 1938.
The Holy Bible, King James Version.

Men Of God Publishing
www.willyounotreason.com

And for those who deny their Lord is the punishment of
Gehenna; and evil is the journey's end.

When they are cast therein, they hear its inhaling as it
boils up,

Almost bursting with rage. Whenever a crowd is cast
therein, the keepers thereof ask them: "Came there not
to you a warner?"

They will say: "Verily, a warner came to us, but we denied
and said: "God has not sent down anything; you are only
in great error."

And they will say: "Had we listened, or used reason, we
would not be among the companions of the Inferno."

And they will confess their transgression: — "So away
with the companions of the Inferno!"

Those who fear their Lord unseen, they have forgiveness
and a great reward.

The Qur'an: A Complete Revelation
(67:6-12)

CONTENTS

ACKNOWLEDGMENTS

In the name of God, the Almighty, the Merciful. Thanks be to God for guiding me and granting me His provision so I could complete this task. Thanks to my brother in faith, Sam Gerrans, for his advice and support in the commission of this work.

> God burdens not a soul save to its capacity; it has what it earned, and it answers for what it acquired. "Our Lord: take Thou us not to task if we forget or commit offence. Our Lord: lay Thou not upon us a burden as Thou didst lay upon those before us. Our Lord: give Thou us not to bear what we have not strength for. And excuse Thou us, and forgive Thou us, and have Thou mercy upon us; Thou art our protector. And help Thou us against the people of the false claimers of guidance."
> (2:286)

FOREWORD

Said Mirza has done the community of Qur'an-believers a great service by compiling the verses and providing the expositions which comprise this book.

I believe this volume will serve as a frequent resource for those who wish to access core Qur'anic teachings on a wide range of subjects, be they debaters, general students, or scholars.

Importantly, Brother Mirza's work provides guidance taken from the Book of Guidance to help the believer live his life in accordance with what the Qur'an itself teaches, and thereby be better placed to give answer to God on the Day of Judgment and, God willing, receive a high reward in the Garden.

I am pleased to recommend this work to all who have an interest in the message of the Qur'an.

Sam Gerrans
Author of *The Qur'an: A Complete Revelation*
quranite.com

INTRODUCTION

The Qur'an claims to be God's revelation, inspired to the Prophet Muhammad, as a final message for all mankind. Sadly, Muslims, those who most loudly proclaim to hold to the Qur'an, do not understand its message.

I have conducted a sincere and honest study of the Qur'an and have concluded that it can only be from God, the Lord of all creation. The Qur'an is clear, complete, and fully detailed. It warns those who have set up false gods and divided God's doctrine into various religions or sects that they will continue to be humiliated in this life — and severely punished in the Hereafter — unless they repent and turn to the One True God.

In this work, I present God's various arguments for His existence, power, and glory. The creation of the sky and the earth, the sun and the moon, and the male and the female are sufficient proofs of God's benevolence, might and majesty.

The religion of Islam claims to take the Qur'an as foundational scripture but the fact of the matter is that the majority of its doctrinal pillars are not found in the Qur'an. Muslims use the *hadith* — alleged sayings of the Prophet Muhammad — to justify their invented practices when the Qur'an is clear that it alone is *the* source of guidance. Muslims, however, cannot accept this fact because it would involve abandoning the dogma, practices and superstitions of their ancestral religion.

The Qur'an does not contain a blueprint of a religion. God calls all men to believe in Him, the last Day and to serve God alone. God chastises the leaders of all religions of abandoning His scriptures and twisting His words in order to divert men from His straight path.

God promises those who believe in His doctrine and do good works their just rewards in the Hereafter. He calls us to take Him as our only

Ally and Protector. He invites all men to carefully consider the Qur'an and to ponder His message carefully. He commands man to use reason — His greatest gift bestowed upon man — to arrive at the true conclusion: that there is one God, without any partners, who created all beings to serve Him alone.

The Qur'an gives us the reality of this life: an exercise in deception, boasting, and competition for increase; it is fragile and fleeting. True life awaits after death. So let us strive for God's acceptance and the attainment of the Garden in the Hereafter; a believer's ultimate goal.

In this work, I have used the excellent translation of the Qur'an titled *The Qur'an: A Complete Revelation* by Sam Gerrans and give him credit for the many ideas and concepts in my work. I invite the interested reader to read his translation of the Qur'an at *reader.quranite.com*.

As a believer, it is my sacred duty to call people to God and I have written this book solely for this purpose. It is my ardent hope that the sincere student will do his own due diligence on the Qur'an and, if God wills, be gifted with an unshakable faith in God alone so he can truly serve the Lord of all creation.

1
GOD'S PROOFS

The Qur'an uses the word *proof* both for its verses and phenomena around us because they are all proofs of God. These proofs are sufficient testimony to the power and benevolence of the Lord of all creation.

> Means of insight have come to you from your Lord; and whoso sees, it is for his soul; and whoso is blind, it is against it; and: "I am not a custodian over you."
> (6:104)

> Say thou: "Have you considered: if it is from God, then you denied it — who is further astray than one who is in extreme schism?"
> We will show them Our proofs in the horizons, and in themselves, until it becomes clear to them that it is the truth. Does it not suffice concerning thy Lord that He is witness to all things?
> (41:53)

> We created man from a sperm-drop — a mingling — that We might test him; and We made him hearing and seeing.
> We guided him on the path, be he grateful or be he ungrateful.
> (76:2-3)

God is the Creator and Maintainer of everything. He holds the sky up lest it fall and turns about the day and night. He sends down rain from the sky and brings forth vegetation from the ground. There is no denying this reality once we sincerely reflect on the countless proofs of God around us.

> Say thou: "Look at what is in the heavens and the earth!"
> But the proofs and the warnings avail not a people who
> do not believe.
>   (10:101)

> If thou thinkest that most of them hear or reason — they
> are only as the cattle; nay, they are further astray in
> the path.
>   (25:44)

So let us reason and ponder on the manifest proofs testifying to the One Creator. Did we create ourselves? Were we created by accident or did God create us? Do we grow the seed or does God? Do we cause the rain to fall down from the clouds or does God? Observe the balance and harmony in nature testifying to the One Architect. Is this all really by accident? Not so, it is God who created all.

> And to Him belongs whoso is in the heavens and the
> earth; and those in His presence are not too proud for
> His service, nor do they grow weary,
> They give glory night and day, and they flag not.
> If they have taken gods from the earth who resurrect:
> Were there in them gods save God, they would have been
> corrupted; and glory be to God, the Lord of the Throne,
> above what they describe!
>   (21:19-22)

2
PROOFS IN PAIRS

God, the One, proclaims that He has created everything in pairs. We find these pairs in all of God's creation; the heavens and the earth, the sun and the moon, the male and the female, the day and the night are some of the examples of this fact alluded to in the Qur'an.

> Glory be to Him who created all the pairs of what the earth produces, and of themselves, and of what they know not!
> (36:36)

Since the Qur'an — like all of God's creation —was created (authored) by God, then we would expect it to be paired as well. And this is indeed the case; the Qur'an contains two types of verses, ambiguous and unambiguous, each with a purpose.

> He it is that sent down upon thee the Writ; among it are explicit proofs: they are the foundation of the Writ; and others are ambiguous. Then as for those in whose hearts is deviation: they follow what is ambiguous thereof, seeking the means of denial, and seeking its interpretation. And no one knows its interpretation save God, and those firm in knowledge; they say: "We believe in

4

it; all is from our Lord." But only those of insight take heed. (3:7)

The creation of the Heavens and Earth

God created the Heavens and the Earth (a pair), in a total of six days. He details how He completed the various tasks in an interval of two days (a pair).[1]

> God is He who created the heavens and the earth and what is between them in six days, then established Himself upon the Throne. You have not, besides Him, any ally or intercessor. Will you then not take heed!
> He directs the matter from the heaven to the earth; then it rises to Him in a day the measure whereof is a thousand years of what you count.
> That is the Knower of the Unseen and the Seen, the Exalted in Might, the Merciful,
> Who made good everything He created, and began the creation of man from clay;
> (32:4-7)

> Your Lord is God, who created the heavens and the earth in six days, then established Himself upon the Throne. He covers the night, the day hastening after it swiftly, and the sun and the moon and the stars are subject by His command. In truth, His are the creation and the command. Blessed be God, the Lord of All Creation!
> (7:54)

> Your Lord is God, who created the heavens and the earth in six days, then established Himself upon the Throne, directing the matter. There is no intercessor save after His leave; that is God, your Lord, so serve Him. Will you then not take heed! (10:3)

1 Of course, Science claims that the universe was created over billions of years. But, it also claims that apes are our cousins (since man and ape evolved from a common ancestor).

And He it is that created the heavens and the earth in six days, — and His Throne was upon the water — that He might try you, which of you is best in deed. And if thou sayest: "You will be raised up after death," those who ignore warning will say: "This is only obvious sorcery."
(11:7)

Who created the heavens and the earth and what is between them in six days, then established Himself upon the Throne — the Almighty — so ask thou about it one aware.
(25:59)

And We created the heavens and the earth and what is between them in six days, and there touched Us no weariness.
(50:38)

During the first two days, God created the Heaven and the Earth as a single mass and then split them apart. In the next two days, He made the mountains and the rivers in the Earth and decreed its nourishment. During the last two days, God commanded the Heaven and the Earth to come together and split the Heaven into seven heavens, decreed the function of each Heaven and then ascended onto His Throne.

Have not those who ignore warning considered that the heavens and the earth were stitched together, then We ripped them apart and made of water every living thing? Will they then not believe!
And We made in the earth firm mountains lest it sway with them; and We made therein mountain passes as ways, that they might be guided;
And We made the sky a roof protected; but they, from its proofs, are turning away.
(21:30-32)

And the earth, We spread it out and cast therein firm
mountains, and caused to grow therein every balanced
thing,
And We made therein livelihoods, for you and those for
whom you are not providers.
And of any thing, with Us only are the treasuries thereof;
and We send it down only in known measure.
(15:19-21)

He created the heavens without pillars you can see, and
He cast into the earth firm mountains lest it sway with
you, and He spread therein every creature. And We sent
down water from the sky, and caused to grow therein
every noble kind.
(31:10)

Say thou: "Do you deny Him who created the earth in two
days, and make equals to Him?" That is the Lord of All
Creation,
And He made therein firm mountains above it, and blessed
it, and decreed therein its diverse nourishment in four
days, equal to the askers.
Then He directed Himself to the sky when it was smoke,
and said to it and to the earth: "Come, willingly or unwillingly." They said: "We come willingly."
And He determined them — seven heavens in two days
— and instructed each heaven in its command. And We
adorned the lower heaven with lamps and as protection.
That is the determination of the Exalted in Might, the
Knowing.
(41:9-12)

He it is that created for you all that is in the earth; then He
directed Himself to the sky and fashioned them seven
heavens; and He knows all things.
(2:29)

And He cast into the earth firm mountains lest it sway
with you; and rivers and ways, that you might be guided;
(16:15)

Have they not looked at the sky above them: — how We
have built it, and made it fair, and it has no rifts?
And the earth: — We spread it out, and cast therein firm
mountains; and We caused to grow therein every delightsome kind
As means of insight and a reminder for every repenting
servant.
(50:6-8)

Pairs throughout the Qur'an

Once we start noticing pairs in God's creation we marvel at the sheer
number of references to pairs in the Qur'an. I have selected a few verses
from various places in the Qur'an which leave no doubt that the Qur'an
is authored by God; He who created everything in pairs.

God, there is no god save He, *the Living, the Eternal. Neither slumber nor sleep* overtakes Him; to Him belongs
what is in the heavens and what is in the earth — who
will intercede with Him save by His leave? *He knows*
what is *before them* and what is *after them,* and *they
encompass not anything of His knowledge save what He
wills.* His Throne overspreads *the heavens and the earth,*
and the preservation thereof wearies Him not; and He
is *the Exalted, the Great.*
(2:255)

Say thou: "O God, Master of Dominion: *Thou givest dominion* to whom Thou wilt, and *Thou removest dominion*
from whom Thou wilt; *Thou exaltest* whom Thou wilt,
and *Thou abasest* whom Thou wilt. In Thy hand is good;
Thou art over all things powerful.

"Thou makest the night enter into the day, and Thou makest the day enter into the night; and Thou bringest forth the living from the dead, and Thou bringest forth the dead from the living. And Thou givest provision to whom Thou wilt without reckoning."

(3:26-27)

Praise belongs to God, to whom belongs *what is in the heavens* and *what is in the earth* — and *to Him belongs the praise in the Hereafter;* and He is *the Wise, the Aware.*

He knows *what penetrates the earth* and *what comes forth from it,* and *what descends from the sky* and *what ascends into it;* and He is *the Merciful, the Forgiving.*

And *those who ignore warning* say: *"The Hour will not come* to us." Say thou: "Verily, by my Lord — *it will come* to you — the Knower of the Unseen!" Not absent from Him is the weight of an atom *in the heavens* or *in the earth,* or *what is smaller* than that *or greater,* save is in a clear writ,

That He might reward *those who heed warning and do righteous deeds;* those have *pardon and a noble provision.*

And *those who strive against Our proofs, to frustrate:* those have the punishment of a painful scourge.

And those given knowledge *see that what is sent down* to thee from thy Lord is the truth, *and it guides to the path* of the *Exalted in Might, the Praiseworthy.*

(34:1-6)

And God *created you from dust;* then *from a sperm-drop; then made He you pairs.* And no female *bears or gives birth* save with His knowledge. *And life is not prolonged* for one full of years, *nor is his life diminished* save it is in a writ; that is easy for God.

And not alike are the *two seas: one is fresh and sweet,* delicious to drink, and *one is salty and bitter.* And *from each you eat succulent flesh,* and *extract ornaments which you wear.* And thou seest the ships ploughing therein, that *you might seek of His bounty* and that *you might be grateful.*

He makes the night enter into the day, and *makes the day enter into the night,* and *He made subject the sun and the moon,* each running for a stated term. That is God, your Lord: *to Him belongs the dominion;* and *those to whom you call, besides Him, possess not the skin of a date-stone.*

If you call to them, they will not hear your call; and *were they to hear, they would not respond to you.* And on the Day of Resurrection they will deny your ascription of partnership. And none can inform thee like One Aware.
(35:11-14)

And a proof for them is the night: We peel away from it the day, and then are they in darkness.

And the sun: it runs to its resting-place; that is the determination of the *Exalted in Might, the Knowing.*

And the moon: We have determined for it phases, until it returns like the old date-leaf stalk.

It behoves not the sun to reach the moon, nor does the night outstrip the day; and each is in a circuit swimming.
(36:37-40)

He created you from one soul; then *He made from it its mate.* And *He sent down for you of the cattle eight pairs.* He creates you in the wombs of your mothers — *creation after creation* — in three darknesses. That is God, your Lord; to Him belongs the dominion; there is no god save He. How then are you diverted?
(39:6)

The Originator of *the Heavens and the Earth* has made *for you of yourselves pairs,* and *of the cattle pairs;* He creates you thereby — there is nothing like Him — and He is the *Hearer, the Seeing.*
(42:11)

And who created the pairs, all of them, and *made for you
  of ships and cattle* that whereon you ride,
That you might settle yourselves upon their backs; then
  remember the favour of your Lord when you have settled
  yourselves thereon, and say: *"Glory be to Him who made
  this subject for us* when we were not equal to it!
"And *to our Lord are we returning."*

(43:12-14)

Have they not looked at the *sky above them: — how We
  have built it, and made it fair, and it has no rifts?*
And *the earth: — We spread it out, and cast therein firm
  mountains; and We caused to grow therein every delightsome kind*
As means of insight and a reminder for every repenting
  servant.

(50:6-8)

And that it is *He who makes laugh, and makes weep,*
And that it is *He who gives death, and gives life,*
And that *He created the two kinds — the male and the
  female —*
From a sperm-drop when it was emitted,
And that upon Him is *the next creation,*

(53:43-47)

What is in the heavens and the earth gives glory to God;
  and He is *the Exalted in Might, the Wise.*
To Him belongs the dominion of the *heavens and the earth;
  He gives life, and He gives death,* and He is over all things
  powerful.
He is the *First and the Last,* and *the Outer and the Inner;*
  and He knows all things.
He it is that created the heavens and the earth in *six days,
  then established Himself upon the Throne.* He knows *what
  penetrates into the earth,* and *what comes forth from it,*
  and *what descends from the heaven,* and *what ascends*

into it. And *He is with you* wherever you may be; and
God sees what you do.
To Him belongs the dominion of *the heavens and the earth;*
and *to God are matters returned.*
He makes *the night enter into the day,* and makes *the day
enter into the night.* And He knows what is in the *breasts.*
(57:1-6)

Does man think that he is left to no purpose?
Was he not a *sperm-drop* from semen emitted?
Then he was a *clinging thing* — and *He created, and
fashioned,*
And made of it *two kinds, the male and the female.*
Is then He not able *to give life to the dead?*
(75:36-40)

3
PROOFS AROUND US

Proofs In The Heavens And The Earth

He it is that created for you all that is in the earth; then He
directed Himself to the sky and fashioned them seven
heavens; and He knows all things.
(2:29)

In the creation of the heavens and the earth, and the
alternation of night and day, and the ship which runs
in the sea with what benefits men, and what God sent
down of water from the sky then gave life thereby to the
earth after its death, and spread therein every creature,
and in the circulation of the winds and the clouds made
subject between the heaven and the earth are proofs for
people who reason.
(2:164)

In the creation of the heavens and the earth and the
alternation of night and day are proofs for men of
understanding:
Those who remember God, standing and sitting and on
their sides, and reflect upon the creation of the heavens
and the earth: "Our Lord: thou createdst not this to no

purpose. Glory be to Thee! And protect Thou us from the punishment of the Fire!

(3:190-191)

God splits the seed and the kernel; He brings forth the living from the dead and is the bringer-forth of the dead from the living. That is God, — how then are you deluded? —

The cleaver of daybreak; and He has appointed the night as rest, and the sun and the moon for reckoning. That is the determination of the Exalted in Might, the Knowing.

And He it is that made for you the stars, that you might be guided thereby in the darknesses of the land and the sea; We have set out and detailed the proofs for people who know.

And He it is that produced you from one soul, then a dwelling-place and a repository[...]. And We have set out and detailed the proofs for people who understand.

And He it is that sends down from the sky water; and We bring forth thereby the growth of all things; and We bring forth from it greenery, bringing forth from it grain heaped up; and from the date-palm, from its spathes, bunches of dates within reach; and gardens of grapevines and olives and pomegranates, similar yet different. Look upon the fruit thereof when it bears fruit and it ripens: in that are proofs for people who believe.

(6:95-99)

Your Lord is God, who created the heavens and the earth in six days, then established Himself upon the Throne. He covers the night, the day hastening after it swiftly, and the sun and the moon and the stars are subject by His command. In truth, His are the creation and the command. Blessed be God, the Lord of All Creation!

(7:54)

And He it is that sends the winds as glad tidings before
His mercy. When they have gathered up heavy clouds,
We drive them to a dead land and send down the water
therein, and bring forth therewith every fruit, — thus
will We bring forth the dead — that you might take heed.
(7:57)

He it is that made the sun an illumination, and the moon
a light; and He determined for it phases, that you might
know the number of years and the reckoning. God created that not save in truth; He sets out and details the
proofs for people who know.
In the alternation of night and day, and what God has created in the heavens and the earth, are proofs for people
who are in prudent fear.
(10:5-6)

Say thou: "Who provides for you from the heaven and the
earth?" If He who owns the hearing and the sight, and
He who brings forth the living from the dead and brings
forth the dead from the living, and He who directs the
matter — then will they say: "God" — then say thou:
"Will you then not be in prudent fear!"
For that is God, your Lord, the Truth; then what is there
after the truth but error? How then are you diverted?
(10:31-32)

He it is that made for you the night wherein to rest, and the
day, sight-giving; in that are proofs for people who hear.
(10:67)

And how many a proof is there in the heavens and the earth
which they pass by, and from which they turn away!
(12:105)

God it is who raised up the heavens, without pillars you
can see, then established Himself upon the Throne. And

He made subject the sun and the moon, each running
for a stated term. He directs the matter; He sets out
and details the proofs, that you might be certain of the
meeting with your Lord.

And He it is that spread out the earth, and placed therein
firm mountains and rivers; and of every fruit He made
therein two kinds; He covers the night with the day; in
that are proofs for people who reflect.

And in the earth are tracts adjacent to one another; and
gardens of grapevines, and crops, and date-palms with
roots shared and independent — watered with one
water; and some of them We make exceed in food others;
in that are proofs for people who reason.

(13:2-4)

He it is that shows you the lightning as fear and hope, and
produces the heavy clouds.

And the thunder gives glory with His praise, as do the
angels, in fear of Him. And He sends the thunderbolts,
and strikes therewith whom He wills. And they dispute
concerning God; and He is strong in assault.

(13:12-13)

And We have set in the sky constellations, and made them
fair for the beholders,

And guarded them from every accursed satan

Save such as steals a hearing; and a clear flame follows him.

And the earth, We spread it out and cast therein firm
mountains, and caused to grow therein every balanced
thing,

And We made therein livelihoods, for you and those for
whom you are not providers.

And of any thing, with Us only are the treasuries thereof;
and We send it down only in known measure.

And We sent the fecundating winds, and sent down water
from the sky, and gave it to you to drink; and it is not
you who are its treasurers.

And We give life, and We give death; and We are the
   inheritor.
(15:16-23)

He it is that sends down from the sky water for you; from
   it is drink; and from it are plants in which you put out
   to pasture;
He causes to grow for you thereby the crops, and the olives,
   and the date-palms, and the grapevines, and every fruit.
   In that is a proof for people who reflect.
(16:10-11)

And We appointed the night and the day as two proofs;
   and We erase the proof of the night and make the proof
   of day sight-giving, that you might seek favour of your
   Lord, and that you might know the number of years
   and the reckoning; and everything have We set out and
   detailed with full explanation.
(17:12)

(Who made the earth for you as a bed, and inserted roads
   for you therein; and sent down from the sky water, and
   thereby have We brought forth diverse kinds of plants:
"Eat, and pasture your cattle." In that are proofs for possessors of intelligence.
Therefrom did We create you, and thereto will We return
   you, and therefrom will We bring you forth another
   time.)
(20:53-55)

Have not those who ignore warning considered that the
   heavens and the earth were stitched together, then We
   ripped them apart and made of water every living thing?
   Will they then not believe!
And We made in the earth firm mountains lest it sway
   with them; and We made therein mountain passes as
   ways, that they might be guided;

And We made the sky a roof protected; but they, from its proofs, are turning away.

And He it is that created the night and the day, and the sun and the moon, each in a circuit swimming.

(21:30-33)

For it is that God makes the night enter into the day, and makes the day enter into the night; and that God is hearing and seeing!

For it is that God, He is the Truth; and that that to which they call besides Him, it is vanity; and that God, He is the Exalted, the Great!

Dost thou not see that God sends down from the sky water, and the earth becomes green? God is subtle and aware.

To Him belongs what is in the heavens and what is in the earth. And God, He is the Free from Need, the Praiseworthy.

(22:61-64)

And We have created above you seven paths, and We are not heedless of the creation.

And We sent down from the sky water in measure, and gave it lodging in the earth — and We are able to take it away —

And We produced for you therewith gardens of date-palms and grapevines — for you therein is much fruit, and thereof you eat —

(23:17-19)

Dost thou not see that God drives the clouds? Then He brings them together; then He makes them a mass, and thou seest the rain come forth from the midst of it. And He sends down from the sky, from mountains therein of hail, and He strikes therewith whom He wills, and turns away therefrom whom He wills. The brilliance of His lightning almost takes away the sight.

God turns about the night and the day; in that is a lesson for those of vision.

And God created every creature from water. And among them is what goes upon its belly, and among them is what goes upon two legs, and among them is what goes upon four. God creates what He wills; God is over all things powerful.

(24:43-45)

Hast thou not considered thy Lord, how He spread the shadow? And had He willed, He would have made it still. Then We made the sun its guide;

Then We took it to Ourselves in an easy taking.

And He it is that appointed for you the night as a covering, and sleep as a rest, and appointed the day as a resurrection.

And He it is that sends the winds as glad tidings at the time of His mercy. And We send down from the sky pure water,

That We might give life thereby to a dead land, and give it as drink to many of what We have created of cattle and men. (25:45-49)

And He it is that loosed the two seas: the one fresh and sweet, and the other salty and bitter, and made between them a barrier, and a complete partition.

(25:53)

Blessed be He who has made in the sky constellations, and made therein a torch, and an illuminating moon.

And He it is that made the night and the day a succession for him who desires to take heed, or desires gratitude.

(25:61-62)

Have they not seen the earth: how much We have caused to grow therein of every noble kind?

In that is a proof, but most of them are not believers.

(26:7-8)

Have they not considered that We made the night that they might rest therein, and the day sight-giving? In that are proofs for people who believe.
(27:86)

God created the heavens and the earth in truth; in that is a proof for the believers.
(29:44)

And if thou askest them: "Who created the heavens and the earth and made subject the sun and the moon?" they will say: "God." How then are they deluded?
God expands provision for whom He wills of His servants, and He straitens for him; God knows all things.
And if thou askest them: "Who sends down water from the sky, and therewith gives life to the earth after its death?" they will say: "God." Say thou: "Praise belongs to God." The truth is, most of them do not reason.
(29:61-63)

Have they not reflected within themselves? God created the heavens and the earth and what is between them only in truth and for a stated term; and many among men are deniers of the meeting with their Lord.
(30:8)

And among His proofs is the creation of the heavens and the earth, and the difference in your tongues and your hues; in that are proofs for all mankind.
And among His proofs is your sleep by night and day, and your seeking of His bounty; in that are proofs for people who hear.
And among His proofs He shows you the lightning as fear and hope, and sends down water from the sky and gives thereby life to the earth after its death; in that are proofs for people who reason.

And among His proofs is that the heaven and the earth
stand by His command; then when He calls you with a
call, from the earth will you then come forth!
And to Him belongs whoso is in the heavens and the earth;
all are to Him humbly obedient.
And He it is that begins creation; then He repeats it — and
it is most easy for Him. And to Him belongs the highest
likeness in the heavens and the earth; and He is the
Exalted in Might, the Wise.
(30:22-27)

And among His proofs is that He sends the winds as bearers of glad tidings, that He might let you taste of His
mercy, and that the ships might run by His command,
and that you might seek of His bounty, and that you
might be grateful.
(And We sent before thee messengers to their people, and
they brought them clear signs; then We took vengeance
on those who were lawbreakers; and it was binding
upon Us to help the believers.)
God is He who sends the winds, that they stir up a cloud,
and He spreads it in the sky as He wills; and He makes
it pieces and thou seest the rain come forth from the
midst of it; then when He makes it fall on whom He wills
of His servants they rejoice
Though they were, before it was sent down upon them
— before that — in despair!
So look thou at the effects of the mercy of God, how He
gives life to the earth after its death: that is the Quickener
of the Dead, and He is over all things powerful.
And if We send a wind, and they see it turn yellow, they
would continue after that to deny.
(30:46-51)

He created the heavens without pillars you can see, and
He cast into the earth firm mountains lest it sway with
you, and He spread therein every creature. And We sent

down water from the sky, and caused to grow therein every noble kind.

(31:10)

Dost thou not see that God makes the night enter into the day, and makes the day enter into the night — and He made subject the sun and the moon, each running to a stated term — and that God is of what you do aware?
For it is that God, He is the Truth, and that that to which they call besides Him is vanity, and that God, He is the Exalted, the Great!
Dost thou not see that the ships run in the sea by the favour of God, that He might show you some of His proofs? In that are proofs for everyone patient and grateful.

(31:29-31)

Have they not considered that We drive the water to the barren land, and bring forth therewith crops whereof their cattle and they themselves eat? Will they then not see!

(32:27)

Do they then not see what is before them, and what following them of the heaven and the earth? If We will, We can make the earth swallow them, or cause to fall upon them pieces of the sky. In that is a proof for every repentant servant.

(34:9)

And not alike are the two seas: one is fresh and sweet, delicious to drink, and one is salty and bitter. And from each you eat succulent flesh, and extract ornaments which you wear. And thou seest the ships ploughing therein, that you might seek of His bounty and that you might be grateful.

(35:12)

God holds the heavens and the earth lest they cease. And
if they should cease, no one could hold them after Him.
He is clement and forgiving.
(35:41)

And a proof for them is the dead earth. We gave it life, and
We brought forth from it grain, then they eat thereof;
And We made therein gardens of date-palms and grape-
vines; and We caused to gush forth therein springs,
That they might eat of its fruit. And their hands made it
not. Will they then not be grateful!
Glory be to Him who created all the pairs of what the earth
produces, and of themselves, and of what they know not!
And a proof for them is the night: We peel away from it
the day, and then are they in darkness.
And the sun: it runs to its resting-place; that is the determination of the Exalted in Might, the Knowing.
And the moon: We have determined for it phases, until it
returns like the old date-leaf stalk.
It behoves not the sun to reach the moon, nor does the
night outstrip the day; and each is in a circuit swimming.
(36:33-40)

And We created not the heaven and the earth and what is
between them to no purpose. That is the assumption of
those who ignore warning. And woe to those who ignore
warning from the Fire!
(38:27)

He created the heavens and the earth in truth. He wraps
the night over the day, and He wraps the day over the
night; and He made subject the sun and the moon, each
running for a stated term. Is He not the Exalted in Might,
the Forgiver?
(39:5)

The creation of the heavens and the earth is greater than
the creation of mankind, but most men know not.
(40:57)

God it is who made for you the earth a fixed lodging, and
the sky a structure, and formed you and made good your
forms, and provided you with good things. That is God,
your Lord; so blessed be God, the Lord of All Creation!
(40:64)

And of His proofs are the night and the day, and the sun
and the moon. Submit not to the sun or the moon, but
submit to God who created them, if it be Him you serve.
(41:37)

And among His proofs is that thou seest the earth laid low,
but when We send down upon it the water, it quivers
and swells. He who gave it life is the Quickener of the
Dead; and He is over all things powerful.
(41:39)

The Originator of the Heavens and the Earth has made
for you of yourselves pairs, and of the cattle pairs; He
creates you thereby — there is nothing like Him — and
He is the Hearer, the Seeing.
(42:11)

And He it is that sends down the rain after they have
despaired, and unfurls His mercy; and He is the Ally,
the Praiseworthy.
And among His proofs is the creation of the heavens and
the earth and what He has spread therein of creatures;
and He has power to gather them when He wills.
(42:28-29)

And among His proofs are the ships in the sea like banners;

If He wills, He calms the wind, and they remain motionless
   on its back — in that are proofs for everyone patient
   and grateful —
Or He wrecks them for what they have earned — but He
   pardons much —
And that those who dispute concerning Our proofs might
   know they have no place of refuge.
(42:32-35)

And if thou askest them who created the heavens and the
   earth, they will say: "There created them the Exalted in
   Might, the Knowing––"
Who made the earth a bed for you, and made roads for
   you therein that you might be guided;
And who sent down water from the sky in measure — and
   We resurrected thereby a dead land; thus will you be
   brought forth —
(43:9-11)

And We created not the heavens and the earth and what
   is between them in play.
We created them not but in truth, but most of them know
   not.
(44:38-39)

In the heavens and the earth are proofs for the believers;
And in your creation and the creatures He scatters in the
   earth are proofs for people who are certain;
And in the alternation of night and day, and in what God
   sends down from the sky of provision and gives life
   thereby to the earth after its death, and in the circulation
   of the winds are proofs for people who reason.
Those are the proofs of God; We recite them to thee in
   truth. Then in what narration after God and His proofs
   will they believe?
(45:3-6)

Have they not looked at the sky above them: — how We
have built it, and made it fair, and it has no rifts?
And the earth: — We spread it out, and cast therein firm
mountains; and We caused to grow therein every delightsome kind
As means of insight and a reminder for every repenting
servant.
(50:6-8)

(And the sky — We built it with might; and We are wealthy!
And the earth — We spread it out; how excellent are
those who level!
And of all things We created two kinds, that you might
take heed.
(51:47-49)

If they were created from nothing: or if they were the
creators:
Or if they created the heavens and the earth: — the truth
is, they are not certain.
If the treasuries of thy Lord are with them: or if they are
the overseers:
Or if they have a stairway on which they can listen in: —
then let their listener come with a clear authority.
(52:35-38)

Have you considered that which you sow?
Is it you who cause it to grow or are We the growers?
If We willed, We could make it debris, and you would
remain bitterly jesting:
"We are debt-laden!
"Nay, we have been deprived!"
Have you considered the water which you drink?
Is it you who sent it down from the rain clouds or are We
the senders?
If We willed, We could make it bitter. Oh, that you were
but grateful!

Have you considered the fire which you light?
Did you produce the tree thereof or were We the producers?
We made it a reminder, and a benefit for the
  desert-travellers.
So give thou glory with the name of thy Lord, the Great!
(56:63-74)

Who created seven heavens in harmony. Thou seest not in
  the creation of the Almighty any imperfection. So return
  thou thy vision: seest thou any rifts?
Then return thou thy vision again and again! Thy sight
  will return to thee humbled and weary.
(67:3-4)

Have We not made the earth a resting-place,
And the mountains as stakes?
And We created you in pairs,
And We made your sleep rest,
And We made the night a garment,
And We made the day a living,
And We built above you seven strong ones,
And We made a blazing torch,
And sent down, from the rain clouds, pouring water,
That We might bring forth thereby grain and plants,
And densely growing gardens.
(78:6-16)

So let man look at his food: —
That We poured water in showers;
Then We split the earth in cracks,
And We caused to grow therein grain,
And grapes, and herbage,
And olives, and date-palms,
And gardens dense with foliage,
And fruits, and grass,
As enjoyment for you and your cattle.
(80:24-32)

Will they then not look at the camels — how they were
　created!
And at the sky — how it was raised!
And at the mountains — how they were erected!
And at the earth — how it was spread out!
(88:17-20)

Everything Submits To God

Is it then other than the doctrine of God they seek, when
　to Him has submitted whoso is in the heavens and the
　earth, willingly or unwillingly, and to Him they will be
　returned?
(3:83)

And to God belongs what is in the heavens and what is in
　the earth, and to God are matters returned.
(3:109)

And to God submits whoso is in the heavens and the
　earth, willingly or unwillingly, as do their shadows in
　the mornings and the evenings.
(13:15)

Have they not seen what things God has created turning
　their shadows to the right and the left in submission to
　God, in all humility?
And to God submits what is in the heavens and what is
　in the earth, among creatures and the angels. And they
　wax not proud;
They fear their Lord above them, and do what they are
　commanded.
(16:48-50)

There is none in the heavens and the earth but comes to
　the Almighty as a servant.)
(19:93)

Dost thou not see that to God submits whoso is in the
heavens, and whoso is in the earth, and the sun, and
the moon, and the stars, and the mountains, and the
trees, and the creatures, and many among mankind?
And upon many has the punishment became binding.
And whom God humiliates, he has none to honour him;
God does what He wills.

(22:18)

And to Him belongs whoso is in the heavens and the earth;
all are to Him humbly obedient.

(30:26)

Man in his ignorance accepted the tremendous responsibility of
free will — to choose between submission or denial of God — with
the result that he will be held accountable on the Day of Judgment for
his actions.

We presented the trust to the heavens and the earth and
the mountains, and they refused to bear it and were
afraid of it; but man bore it — he is unjust and ignorant
—

That God might punish the wavering men, and the wavering women, and the idolaters, and the idolatresses; and
that God might turn towards the believing men and the
believing women. And God is forgiving and merciful.

(33:72-73)

Everything Made Serviceable to us by God

God is He who created the heavens and the earth, and sent
down from the sky water wherewith He brought forth
some fruits as a provision for you; and He made subject
for you the ship to run upon the sea by His command;
and He made subject for you the rivers;

And He made subject for you the sun and the moon, both
constant; and He made subject for you the night and
the day.

And He gives you of all that you ask of Him. And if you
should count the favour of God, you will not calculate
it; man is a wrongdoer and an ingrate.

(14:32-34)

And the cattle, He created them (for you therein are
warmth and benefits; and of them you eat,

And for you therein is comeliness when you bring them
home to rest, and when you take them out to pasture;

And they bear your loads to a land you could not have
reached save with great trouble to yourselves; your
Lord is kind and merciful.)

And horses, and mules, and donkeys for you to ride, and
as adornment; and He creates what you know not.

And upon God is the course of the path; and some of them
deviate. And had He willed, He would have guided you
all together.

He it is that sends down from the sky water for you; from
it is drink; and from it are plants in which you put out
to pasture;

He causes to grow for you thereby the crops, and the olives,
and the date-palms, and the grapevines, and every fruit.
In that is a proof for people who reflect.

And He made subject for you the night, and the day, and
the sun, and the moon; and the stars are made subject
by His command — in that are proofs for people who
reason —

As is what He created for you in the earth of different hues;
in that is a proof for people who take heed.

And He it is that made subject the sea, that you might
eat therefrom fresh flesh, and bring forth therefrom
ornaments which you wear — and thou seest the ships
ploughing therein — and that you might seek of His
bounty, and that you might be grateful.

And He cast into the earth firm mountains lest it sway
  with you; and rivers and ways, that you might be guided;
And landmarks; and by the star are they guided.
Is then He who creates like one who creates not? Will you
  then not take heed!
(16:5-17)

And you have in the cattle a lesson: We give you to drink
  of what is in its bellies — between excreta and blood
  — pure milk, palatable to the drinkers.
And of the fruits of the date-palms and grapevines: you
  take therefrom an intoxicant, and goodly provision. In
  that is a proof for people who reason.
And thy Lord instructed the bee: "Take thou houses of the
  mountains, and of the trees, and of what they construct.
"Then eat thou of every fruit, and follow thou the ways
  of thy Lord gently." There comes out of their bellies a
  drink differing in its hues wherein is healing for men.
  In that is a proof for people who reflect.
(16:66-69)

Have they not considered the birds made subject in the
  air of the sky? There holds them only God; in that are
  proofs for people who believe.
And God made for you from your houses a place of rest;
  and He made for you from the hides of cattle houses
  which you find light on the day of your journey and on
  the day of your sojourn; and of their wool and their fur
  and their hair furnishing and enjoyment for a time.
And God appointed for you of what He has created shades,
  and made for you of the mountains places of refuge, and
  made for you garments to protect you from the heat, and
  garments to protect you from your might. Thus does He
  complete His favour upon you, that you might submit.
(16:79-81)

We have honoured the children of Adam, and carried
  them on land and sea, and provided them with good
  things, and preferred them greatly above many of those
  We created.
(17:70)

Dost thou not see that God made subject for you what
  is in the earth, and the ships run upon the sea by His
  command? And He holds back the sky lest it fall upon
  the earth save by His leave; God is to mankind kind and
  merciful.
(22:65)

And for you in the cattle is a lesson: We give you drink
  of what is in their bellies, and for you therein are many
  benefits; and of them you eat,
And upon them, and upon the ships, are you carried.
(23:21-22)

Have they not considered that We created cattle for them
  of what Our hands made, then are they their masters?
And We subdued them to them, and some of them they
  ride, and some of them they eat;
And they have in them benefits and drinks. Will they then
  not be grateful?
(36:71-73)

God it is who made for you the cattle, that you ride some,
  and some eat
— And you have in them benefits — and that you might
  attain upon them a need in your breasts; and upon them
  and upon the ships are you carried.
And He shows you His proofs; then which of the proofs
  of God do you deny?
(40:79-81)

And who created the pairs, all of them, and made for you
of ships and cattle that whereon you ride,
That you might settle yourselves upon their backs; then
remember the favour of your Lord when you have settled yourselves thereon, and say: "Glory be to Him who
made this subject for us when we were not equal to it!
"And to our Lord are we returning."
(43:12-14)

God it is who made subject for you the sea, that the ships
might run therein by His command, and that you might
seek of His bounty; and that you might be grateful.
And He made subject for you what is in the heavens and
what is in the earth — altogether from Him. In that are
proofs for people who reflect.
(45:12-13)

Would You Really Call to Someone Else?

When confronted with a disaster, we instinctively call to God alone for
help. Try to remember a time when you faced a real crisis. Who did you
call? God tests man with good to see if he is grateful to Him and with
evil to see if he humbles himself to God.

And We divided them in the earth into communities —
some of them righteous, and some of them other than
that — and We tried them with good things and evil
deeds, that they might return.
(7:168)

And when thy Lord brought forth from the children of
Adam, from their backs, their progeny, and made them
bear witness as to themselves: "Am I not your Lord?"
— they said: "Verily, we bear witness." — "Lest you say
on the Day of Resurrection: 'Of this were we unaware,'
(7:172)

Say thou: "Have you considered: if the punishment of God comes upon you, or the Hour comes upon you, will you call to other than God, if you be truthful?"
The truth is, to Him will you call; and He will remove that for which you call to Him if He wills; and you will forget that to which you ascribe a partnership.
(6:40-41)

Say thou: "Have you considered: if God takes away your hearing and your sight and seals your hearts, who is the god save God who will restore it to you?" See thou how We expound the proofs; then they turn away.
(6:46)

Say thou: "Who delivers you from the darknesses of the land and the sea? You call to Him humbly and in secret: 'If He delivers us from this, we will be among the grateful.'"
Say thou: "God delivers you from it and from every distress; then you ascribe a partnership."
Say thou: "He is the one able to send punishment upon you from above you or from beneath your feet, or to confound you through sects and let some of you taste the might of others." See thou how We expound the proofs, that they might understand,
(6:63-65)

He it is that lets you travel in the earth and the sea; when you have boarded ships and sailed by them with a good breeze and exulted thereat–– A tempest wind came upon them, and the waves came on them from every side, and they thought they were encompassed therein; they called to God, sincere to Him in doctrine: "If Thou deliver us from this, we will be among the grateful!"
Then when He delivers them, they rebel in the earth without cause.) O mankind: your sectarian zealotry is but against yourselves, — the enjoyment of the life of this

world — then to Us is your return and We will inform you of what you did.

(10:22-23)

Corruption has appeared on land and sea for what the hands of men have earned, that He might let them taste some of what they have done, that they might return.

(30:41)

And when a wave covers them like canopies they call to God, sincere to Him in doctrine; then when He delivers them to the land, some among them are lukewarm. And none rejects Our proofs but everyone treacherous and ungrateful.

(31:32)

And We will let them taste of the lower punishment before the greater, that they might return.

(32:21)

4
PROOFS IN US

L et us trace the genesis of our creation. God created Adam, the first man, from clay and created his progeny from sperm. This is the truth of how man came to be. God created man in the best form and honored him above many of His creation. Man, truly, has a noble destiny.

Proofs Evident In Man

How can you deny God? When you were dead, He gave
   you life; then will He give you death; then will He give
   you life; then to Him will you be returned.
                     (2:28)

He it is who forms you in the wombs as He wills. There is
   no god save He, the Exalted in Might, the Wise.
                     (3:6)

And He it is that produced you from one soul, then a
   dwelling-place and a repository[...]. And We have set
   out and detailed the proofs for people who understand.
                     (6:98)

Dost thou not see that God created the heavens and the
   earth in truth? If He wills, He will remove you and bring
   a new creation;
And that is not difficult for God. (14:19-20)

He created man from a sperm-drop — and then is he an open disputant.

(16:4)

And God created you; then will He take you. And among you is he who is sent back to the most abject age, so that he knows not, after knowledge, anything. God is knowing and powerful.

And God has favoured some of you over others in provision, but those favoured will not give over their provision to those whom their right hands possess, that they be equal therein; is it then the favour of God they reject?

And God has appointed for you from yourselves wives, and has appointed for you from your wives sons and grandsons, and has provided you of good things. Is it then in vanity that they believe, and the favour of God they deny

And serve rather than God what possesses no provision for them among the heavens or the earth at all, and can do nothing?

(16:70-73)

And God brought you forth from the wombs of your mothers not knowing anything, and appointed for you hearing and sight and hearts, that you might be grateful.

(16:78)

O mankind: if you are in doubt about the Resurrection, then: We created you from dust; then from a sperm-drop; then from a clinging thing; then from a fleshy lump formed and unformed — that We might make plain to you. And We settle in the wombs what We will to a stated term; then We bring you forth as a child; then that you should reach your maturity. And among you is he who is taken. And among you is he who is sent back to the most abject age, so that he knows not, after knowledge, anything. And thou seest the earth lifeless; then when

We send down upon it water it quivers and swells and
grows every delightful kind
For it is that God, He is the Truth; and that He gives life to
the dead; and that He is over all things powerful;
(22:5-6)

And We created man from an extract of clay;
Then We placed him as a sperm-drop in a secure fixed
lodging;
Then We created the sperm-drop a clinging thing, and
created the clinging thing a fleshy lump, and created
the fleshy lump bones, and clothed the bones with flesh;
then We produced it as another creation — and blessed
be God, the best of creators!
Then after that will you die;
Then on the Day of Resurrection will you be raised.
(23:12-16)

And He it is that produced for you hearing and sight and
hearts; little are you grateful.
And He it is that created you in the earth; and to Him will
you be gathered.
And He it is that gives life, and gives death; and His is
the alternation of night and day. Will you then not use
reason!
(23:78-80)

And He it is that created from water a mortal, and made
for him blood relations and marriage relations; and thy
Lord is powerful.
(25:54)

And among His proofs is that He created you from dust;
then are you mortals dispersing!
And among His proofs is that He created for you spouses
from yourselves that you might be reassured thereby,

and made between you love and mercy; in that are proofs
for people who reflect.
(30:20-21)

God is He who created you of weakness, then appointed
He, after weakness, strength; then He appointed, after
strength, weakness and white hair. He creates what He
wills; and He is the Knowing, the Powerful.
(30:54)

Who made good everything He created, and began the
creation of man from clay;
Then He made his progeny of an extraction of despised
water;
Then He fashioned him, and breathed into him of His Spirit;
and He made for you hearing and sight and hearts; little
are you grateful.
(32:7-9)

And God created you from dust; then from a sperm-drop;
then made He you pairs. And no female bears or gives
birth save with His knowledge. And life is not prolonged
for one full of years, nor is his life diminished save it is
in a writ; that is easy for God.
(35:11)

And to whom We give long life, We reverse him in creation.
Will you then not use reason! (36:68)
So ask thou them: are they harder to create, or those We
have created? We created them of clinging clay.
Yet thou dost marvel; and they deride
And, when they are reminded, bear not in mind
And, when they see a proof, turn in derision.
(37:11-14)

He created you from one soul; then He made from it its
mate. And He sent down for you of the cattle eight pairs.

He creates you in the wombs of your mothers — creation
after creation — in three darknesses. That is God, your
Lord; to Him belongs the dominion; there is no god save
He. How then are you diverted?
(39:6)

He it is that created you from dust; then from a sperm-
drop; then from a clinging thing; then He brings you forth
as a child; then that you reach your maturity; then that
you become old — and among you is he who is caused
to die before — and that you reach a stated term, and
that you might use reason.
(40:67)

And in your creation and the creatures He scatters in the
earth are proofs for people who are certain;
(45:4)

And in the earth are proofs for those who are certain,
And in yourselves; do you then not see!
(51:20-21)

We created them, and strengthened their form and, when
We will, We will change their likenesses completely.
(76:28)

Did We not create you from a despised water?
And We placed it in a fixed lodging secure
For a known measure.
So We determined; and how excellent are those who
determine!
Woe, that day, to the deniers!
Have We not made the earth a container
Of the living and the dead?
And We made therein high, firm mountains, and gave you
to drink sweet water.
(77:20-27)

40

Are you harder in creation, or the sky? He built it;
He raised the ceiling thereof, and fashioned it;
And He made dark its night, and brought forth its morning.
And the earth, after that, He spread it out;
He brought forth therefrom its water and its pasture;
And the mountains He set firmly
As enjoyment for you and for your cattle.

(79:27-33)

O man: what deluded thee concerning thy Lord, the Noble,
Who created thee and fashioned thee and proportioned
thee in balance,
In what form He willed assembling thee?

(82:6-8)

5
PROOFS OF RESURRECTION

God requires us to believe in a life after death. While most men claim to believe in a Resurrection, their actions betray their true belief. If men sincerely believed in a Day of Judgment, would they waste their limited time in pointless activities? Would they oppress others and do evil? The fact of the matter is that most men do not believe that they will stand before God to give a full account of their deeds in this life.

> That no bearer of burdens bears the burden of another,
> And that man has not save that for which he strove,
> And that his striving will be seen
> — Then will he be rewarded with the fullest reward —
> (53:38-41)

If this temporary life requires so much struggle, sacrifice and hardship, how can it be that we can attain the eternal Garden in the Hereafter simply by going to a place of worship once a week? The labors required to attain the Garden must be much more strenuous. Judgment Day is coming and only those who strive for the Garden with all their energy and resources will be successful.

> God has bought from the believers their lives and their
> wealth; for that the Garden is theirs — they fighting in

the cause of God, killing and being killed — a promise binding upon Him in the Torah and the Gospel and the Qur'an. And who better fulfils his covenant than God? Rejoice then in your bargain that you have contracted with Him; and that is the Great Achievement.

(9:111)

Men doubt the Hereafter because they have never seen the dead come to life, and because they do not wish to be held accountable for their actions. God answers the first doubt by highlighting the undeniable fact that He has already created us. Surely, repeating an act is much easier than initiating it. He answers the second doubt by stating that He did not create the heavens and the earth to no purpose; and if there be any purpose to them at all then surely the doers of good and evil must be given their just rewards.[2] Yet, more often than not, evil men live a good life and die a good death. Thus, it is necessary that man be resurrected so that he be paid back in full for his actions — if God is Just and has created the universe for a purpose (both of which are true). Thus, Judgment is a logical necessity.

God directs our attention to His ceaseless creation and destruction of vegetation. He sends the fertilizing wind and life-giving rain to resurrect the dead land; observe how it revives and springs forth at the command of God. The land is decked out in beauty and greenery for a time. Then when God's command comes, He makes it scattered debris. Thus is the Resurrection.

Proofs Of Resurrection

And they swear by God their strongest oaths: "God will not raise up him who dies." Verily, it is a promise binding upon Him, — but most men know not —
That He might make plain to them that wherein they differ, and that those who ignore warning might know that they were liars.

(16:38-39)

---

2 I give credit to Brother Gerrans for this point.

And God sends down from the sky water and gives life
thereby to the earth after its death. In that is a proof
for people who hear.
(16:65)

And they say: "When we are bones and dust, will we be
raised up as a new creation?"
Say thou: "Be you stones or iron
"Or a creation of what is great within your breasts!" And
they will say: "Who will bring us back?" Say thou: "He
who created you the first time." Then they will shake
their heads at thee and say: "When is it?" Say thou: "It
may be that it is near:
"The day He will call you, and you will answer with His
praise, and you will think that you tarried only a little."
(17:49-52)

And whom God guides, he is guided; and whom He sends
astray, for them thou wilt find no allies besides Him.
And We will gather them on the Day of Resurrection on
their faces — blind and dumb and deaf — their shelter
is Gehenna; whenever it subsides, We will increase for
them an inferno.
That is their reward because they denied Our proofs and
said: "When we are bones and dust, will we be raised
up as a new creation?"
Have they not considered that God, who created the heavens and the earth, has power to create the like of them?
And He has made for them a term whereof there is no
doubt; but the wrongdoers refuse save denial.
(17:97-99)

And man says: "When I am dead, am I then to be brought
forth alive?"
Does not man remember that We created him before,
when he was nothing?
(19:66-67)

And He it is that gave you life; then will He give you death;
then will He give you life. Man is an ingrate.
(22:66)

(Have they not seen how God originates creation, then
repeats it? That is easy for God.
Say thou: "Travel in the earth and see how He originated
creation; then will God produce the latter creation; God
is over all things powerful.
(29:19-20)

God begins creation; then He repeats it; then to Him will
you be returned.
(30:11)

He brings forth the living from the dead, and brings forth
the dead from the living, and He gives life to the earth
after its death; and thus will you be brought forth.
(30:19)

And God is He who sends the winds, that they stir up a
cloud; and We drive it to a dead land, and give life thereby
to the earth after its death. Thus is the Resurrection.
(35:9)

Has man not considered that We created him from a
sperm-drop? And then is he an open disputant.
And he strikes for Us a similitude, and forgets his creation;
he says: "Who will give life to the bones when they are
rotted away?"
Say thou: "He will give them life who produced them the
first time," — and He knows all creation —
"Who made for you from the green tree fire, and then
therefrom you kindle."
Is not He who created the heavens and the earth able to
create the like of them? Verily; and He is the Knowing
Creator.

His command, when He intends a thing, is that He says to it: "Be thou," and it is.
(36:77-82)

Say thou: "God gives you life; then He gives you death; then will He gather you to the Day of Resurrection whereof there is no doubt; but most men know not."
(45:26)

Have they not considered that God — who created the heavens and the earth and was not wearied by their creation — is able to give life to the dead? Verily, He is over all things powerful.
(46:33)

The truth is, they marvel that a warner has come to them from among them. And the false claimers of guidance say: "This is an amazing thing:
"When we are dead and become dust[...]? That is a far return!"
We know what the earth diminishes of them. And with Us is a preserving Writ.
The truth is, they denied the truth when it came to them, so they are in a confused state.
Have they not looked at the sky above them: — how We have built it, and made it fair, and it has no rifts?
And the earth: — We spread it out, and cast therein firm mountains; and We caused to grow therein every delightsome kind
As means of insight and a reminder for every repenting servant.
And We sent down from the sky blessed water, and caused to grow thereby gardens and the grain of harvest,
And tall date-palms with spathes in layers
As a provision for the servants. And therewith gave We life to a dead land. Thus will be the Emergence.
(50:2-11)

Were We then wearied by the first creation? Yet they are
in doubt about a new creation.
(50:15)

And that it is He who gives death, and gives life,
And that He created the two kinds — the male and the
female —
From a sperm-drop when it was emitted,
And that upon Him is the next creation,
(53:44-47)

We created you. Oh, that you but gave credence!
Have you considered what you emit?
Did you create it or are We the creators?
We have decreed death among you; and We will not be
outrun,
That We will change your likenesses, and produce you in
what you know not.
And you have known the former creation. Oh, that you
but took heed!
(56:57-62)

Know that God gives life to the earth after its death. We
have made plain the proofs to you, that you might use
reason.
(57:17)

Those who ignore warning claim that they will never be
raised. Say thou: "Verily, by my Lord, you will be raised!
Then will you be informed of what you did; and that is
easy for God."
(64:7)

Does man think that We will not assemble his bones?
Verily, We are able to fashion his fingertips.
The truth is, man intends to continue unrestrained;
(75:3-5)

Does man think that he is left to no purpose?
Was he not a sperm-drop from semen emitted?
Then he was a clinging thing — and He created, and
   fashioned,
And made of it two kinds, the male and the female.
Is then He not able to give life to the dead?
(75:36-40)

So let man look from what he was created:
He was created from a gushing water,
Issuing forth from between the loins and the breast-bones.
He is able to return him.
(86:5-8)

6
PROOFS OF THE QUR'AN

The Qur'an cannot be tampered with. We can verify this by considering that Muslims, the inheritors of the Qur'an, were unable to change or modify it to support most of their religion. Such is the divine protection of this message that they had to invent an entirely separate *hadith* literature — alleged sayings of the Prophet Muhammad — to explain the various requirements and practices that are the basis of their invented religion.

> Those who deny the remembrance when it has come to
> them[...]. And it is a mighty Writ
> — Falsehood cannot reach it from before it or from after
> it — a revelation from One wise and praiseworthy.
> (41:41-42)

> We sent down the remembrance, and We are its custodian.
> (15:9)

> The truth is, it is a glorious recitation,
> In a protected tablet.
> (85:21-22)

The Qur'an is in Arabic and a unique feature of this language is that most words are based on a three letter root;[3] which has a core meaning. This makes it very difficult to change the meaning of a word, since the meanings of other words based on the same root would have to be changed as well. Over time, Muslims have altered the meanings of keywords in the Qur'an to lend support to their various invented rituals and dogmas but we can always retrieve the original meaning of a keyword by looking at other words which share the same root in the Qur'an.[4] The Qur'an also uses keywords in varying contexts to frustrate those who are bent on corrupting the word of God. Muslims are not the first to have changed the meanings of words in their Scripture; the Jews did the same with the Torah.

> Do you hope that they[5] will believe you? And a faction among them had heard the word of God, then twisted it after they had understood it, when they knew.
> (2:75)

> So for their violation of their agreement We cursed them and made their hearts hard. They twist words from their places, and have forgotten a portion of that they were reminded of. And thou wilt not cease to find treachery among them save a few among them; but pardon thou them, and forbear thou; God loves the doers of good.
> (5:13)

Muslims were able to change the meanings of words in the Qur'an, using sectarian definitions and references to *hadith* literature, in order to attach the *religion of Islam* to the Qur'an. They were, however, unable to change the text of the Qur'an. Those who investigate the Qur'an carefully can see their deceptions plainly. For example, the Islamic religion claims that *salaat* — mentioned multiple times in the Qur'an — means *to perform a specific ritual facing the Kaaba in Mecca.* However, the details of this important ritual[6] are conspicuously absent in

---

3 Further elaboration to follow in Chapter 9.
4 I am thankful to brother Gerrans for this insight.
5 The Jews.
6 Muslims string together terms such as sujud and rukuh in the Qur'an to justify this ritual

the Qur'an. Muslims counter by saying that its details are found in the *hadith* literature. But this contradicts the Qur'an's claim that it is clear, complete, and fully detailed.

> "Is it other than God I should seek as judge when He it is
> that sent down to you the Writ set out and detailed?"
> And those to whom We gave the Writ know that it is
> sent down from thy Lord with the truth; so be thou not
> of those who doubt.
> (6:114)

> A Writ the proofs whereof are set out and detailed, an
> Arabic recitation for people who know,
> As a bearer of glad tidings and a warner; but most of them
> turn away, so they hear not.
> (41:3-4)

God's Challenge

> O mankind: serve your Lord who created you, and those
> before you, that you might be in prudent fear;
> Who made the earth for you a couch, and the sky a struc-
> ture, and sent down from the sky water, then brought
> forth thereby fruits as provision for you; so make not
> equals to God when you know.
> And if you are in doubt about what We have sent down
> upon Our servant, then bring a sūrah the like thereof;
> and call your witnesses other than God, if you be truthful.
> But if you do not — and you will not — then be in prudent
> fear of the Fire, whose fuel is men and stones, prepared
> for the false claimers of guidance.
> (2:21-24)

The Arabic word *sūrah* means *a chapter*. Lane's lexicon defines it as: "Eminence, or nobility: rank or station: Hence its application in relation to the Ḳur-án, [to signify A chapter thereof,] because each of

---

but the fact remains that this ritual, in its entirety, is not found in the Qur'an. See Chapter 13.

what are thus called forms one degree, or step, distinct from another, or [leading] to another". We find confirmation of this definition in the Qu'ran in the beginning of Chapter 24.

> A sūrah We have sent down and made obligatory, and
>   wherein We sent down clear proofs, that you might
>   take heed:
> (24:1)

Now that we have established that the word *surah* means a *chapter*, we come back to the challenge itself which is repeated again, in a slightly different manner, in Chapter 10.

> And this Qur'an is not such as could be invented by other
>   than God; but it is a confirmation of what is before it,
>   and an exposition of the Writ about which there is no
>   doubt, from the Lord of All Creation.
> If they say: "He invented it," say thou: "Bring a sūrah the
>   like thereof; and call whom you can besides God, if you
>   be truthful."
> (10:37-38)

The third and final instance of this challenge is found in Chapter 11 of the Qur'an and this time God challenges the Qur'an's skeptics to bring ten chapters like this chapter.

> If they say: "He has invented it," then say thou: "Then bring
>   ten sūrahs the like thereof, invented; and call to whom
>   you can, besides God, if you be truthful."
> And if they respond not to you, then know that it is but
>   sent down with the knowledge of God, and that there is
>   no god save He — so will you be submitting?
> (11:13-14)

Muslims' understanding of this challenge is wrong; they think it means that God is challenging skeptics to produce an Arabic work similar to a chapter in the Qur'an. However, there are a number of problems with this interpretation. Firstly, the challenge is to all of mankind, this means that a skeptic is free to produce a similar chapter in his own language i.e. he does not have to match the stylistic quality of the Arabic in the Qur'an. Secondly, no objective criteria — by which an attempt could be judged — are mentioned in this challenge, and absent strict objective criteria, it is all but impossible to render a verdict.

The absence of any objective criteria in God's challenge has emboldened doubters of the Qur'an to state that this challenge is not really a challenge i.e. what is the big deal? Muslims' only defense is that the Qur'an is in superior Arabic prose and the challenge is to match the Qur'anic style in terms of its stylistic beauty. However, as discussed earlier, the challenge is to all of mankind, therefore, the stylistic quality of the Arabic in the Qur'an is irrelevant.

> And if you are in doubt about what We have sent down
> upon Our servant, then bring a sūrah the like thereof;
> and call your witnesses other than God, if you be truthful.
> (2:23)

If we examine the above verse carefully we notice a further nuance to the challenge; it is not to simply bring a text claiming to be from God but to bring witnesses attesting to this claim; something which Joseph Smith — the founder of Mormonism — managed to do. This false religion considers "The Book of Mormon" to be a divinely revealed text. In the introduction of this text, we find a testification by three witnesses[7] that this text is a true translation by Mr. Smith of engravings upon plates which an angel of God brought down from heaven.[8]

So, has the challenge by God to mankind been met? Joseph Smith has created a work which men testified to be from God. If we understand God's challenge to mean bringing witnesses testifying that an invented text is from God then, yes, it has been met; but, as we shall see, there is a final nuance to God's challenge.

---

7 A further eight witnesses testified to this claim as well.
8 Smith, Joseph. The Book of Mormon. Church Of Jesus Christ Of Latterday Saints, 1920.

> And if you are in doubt about what We have sent down
> upon Our servant, then bring a sūrah the like thereof;
> and *call your witnesses other than God,* if you be truthful.
> (2:23)

The key to understanding God's challenge, and realizing that it can never be met, is the statement "and call your witnesses other than God"; God is challenging the doubters of the Qur'an to bring witnesses *besides Himself* for a reason. It is because God has already testified to sending down the Qur'an to prophet Muhammad with His knowledge. Therefore, God's challenge cannot and will never be met because it does not matter how many witnesses testify that an invented text is from God. God has already testified that the Qur'an is from Him, and His testimony trumps all testimonies.

> But God bears witness to what He has sent down to thee:
> He sent it down with His knowledge; and the angels bear
> witness, but sufficient is God as witness.
> (4:166)

God's challenge is a *logical* checkmate to the doubters of the Qur'an's divinely revealed nature — and a warning from God.

> But if you do not — *and you will not* — then be in prudent
> fear of the Fire, whose fuel is men and stones, prepared
> for the false claimers of guidance.
> (2:24)

In summary, God's challenge to a skeptic is to create his own text and to bring witnesses attesting that his invented text is from God; and even if he does that, he still fails to win his case because the testimony of his accomplices can never stand up to God's True testimony. Therefore, it is a logical impossibility to best God's challenge.

The fact that most people do not understand God's challenge is itself alluded to in the next verse after the second instance of God's challenge.

If they say: "He invented it," say thou: "Bring a sūrah the like thereof; and call whom you can besides God, if you be truthful."

The truth is, they have denied what they compassed not in knowledge, and whose interpretation has not yet come to them. Thus denied those before them. Then see thou how was the final outcome of the wrongdoers.
(10:38-39)

God's Arguments for the Qur'an's Divine Origin

(Will they then not consider the Qur'an with care! And had it been from other than God, they would have found therein much contradiction.)
(4:82)

And they measured God not with the measure due Him when they said: "God has not sent down upon a mortal anything." Say thou: "Who sent down the Writ which Moses brought as a light and guidance for men?" (You make it into parchments which you show; and you conceal much; and you were taught what you knew not, you and your fathers.) Say thou: "God"; then leave thou them playing in their vain discourses.
(6:91)

And if thou art in doubt about what We have sent down to thee, then ask thou those who read the Writ before thee. The truth from thy Lord has come to thee, so be thou not of those who doubt.
(10:94)

(If they say: "He has invented it," say thou: "If I have invented it, then upon me is my crime — but I am quit of what you commit.")
(11:35)

And there prevented men from believing when the guidance came to them only that they said: "Has God raised up a mortal as messenger?"

Say thou: "Had there been in the earth angels walking securely, We would have sent down upon them from the sky an angel as messenger."

(17:94-95)

And they say: "Oh, that he would but bring us a proof from his Lord!" Has there not come to them clear evidence of what is in the former scriptures?

And had We destroyed them with a punishment before him, they would have said: "Our Lord: oh, that Thou hadst but sent to us a messenger, so we might have followed Thy proofs before we were humiliated and disgraced!"

Say thou: "All are waiting — so wait; and you will come to know who are the companions of the even path, and who is guided."

(20:133-135)

Have they then not considered the word with care? If there has come to them what came not to their fathers of old,

Or if they did not know their messenger, and so do not recognise him,

Or if they say: "He is possessed," — the truth is, he has brought them the truth, but most of them are averse to the truth.

And had the truth followed their vain desires, the heavens and the earth and whoso is therein would have been corrupted; the truth is, We brought them their remembrance, and they from their remembrance are turning away.

(23:68-71)

We have sent down manifest proofs; and God guides whom He wills to a straight path. (24:46)

And it is a revelation of the Lord of All Creation,
Brought down by the Faithful Spirit
Upon thy heart — that thou be of the warners —
In a clear Arabic tongue.
And it is in the writings of the former peoples.
Is it not a proof to them that the learned of the children
of Israel know it?

(26:192-197)

When they have come, He will say: "Did you deny My
proofs, when you had not encompassed them in knowledge? Or what was it you did?"

(27:84)

And were it not that calamity should befall them because
of what their hands sent ahead[...]. Then will they say:
"Our Lord: oh, that Thou hadst but sent for us a messenger, then would we have followed Thy proofs and
been among the believers!"
But when there came to them the truth from Us, they said:
"Oh, that he were but given the like of what was given
to Moses!" Do they not deny what was given to Moses
before? They say: "Two sorceries supporting each other."
And they say: "We are deniers of both."
Say thou: "Then bring a writ from God that gives better
guidance than these: I will follow it, if you be truthful."

(28:47-49)

And they say: "Oh, that proofs were but sent down upon
him from his Lord!" Say thou: "The proofs are only with
God, and I am only a clear warner."
Does it not suffice them that We have sent down upon
thee the Writ recited to them? In that is a mercy and a
reminder for people who believe.

(29:50-51)

And We have struck for mankind in this Qur'an every
similitude, that they might take heed;

An Arabic recitation, free of deviation, that they might be
in prudent fear.

(39:27-28)

And they said: "Oh, that this Qur'an had but been sent
down upon a great man of the two cities!"

Is it they who distribute the mercy of thy Lord? We have
distributed among them their livelihood in the life of this
world and raised some of them above others in degree,
that some of them might take others in service; but the
mercy of thy Lord is better than what they amass.

(43:31-32)

And when Our proofs are recited to them as clear signs,
those who ignore warning say of the truth when it has
come to them: "This is obvious sorcery."

If they say: "He has invented it," say thou: "If I have invented
it, then you will not possess for me anything against God.
He best knows what you say concerning it; sufficient
is He as witness between me and you"; and He is the
Forgiving, the Merciful.

Say thou: "I am no new thing among the messengers,
and I know not what will be done with me or with you.
I follow only what is revealed to me; and I am only a
clear warner."

Say thou: "Have you considered: if it be from God and you
deny it, and a witness bore witness among the children
of Israel to the like thereof, and he believed when you
have waxed proud[...]?" God guides not the wrongdoing
people.

And those who ignore warning say of those who heed
warning: "Had it been good, they would not have preceded us to it." And when they are not guided by it, then
they will say: "This is an ancient falsehood."

But before it was the Writ of Moses a model and a mercy;
and this is a confirming Writ, in an Arabic tongue, that it
might warn those who do wrong, and bring glad tidings
to the doers of good:

(46:7-12)

Will they then not consider the Qur'an with care! If there
be locks upon their hearts:

(47:24)

Thus came there no messenger to those before them save
they said: "A sorcerer, or one possessed."
Have they passed it down? The truth is, they are a people
transgressing all bounds.

(51:52-53)

Or if they say: "He has invented it," — the truth is, they
do not believe.
Then let them produce a narrative the like thereof, if they
be truthful.

(52:33-34)

Do you then marvel at this narrative,
And laugh, and not weep,
While you are puffed up in heedlessness?
But submit to God, and serve.

(53:59-62)

7
THE TRUE FAITH

According to the Qur'an, the true faith has nothing to with following a specific religion. It is to submit completely to God; to acknowledge His total sovereignty. It is to take Him as one's only Ally and Protector, and to serve Him alone. This is a far cry from the teachings of today's sectarian religions

> The doctrine with God is submission. And those given the Writ differed only after knowledge had come to them, through sectarian zealotry between them; and whoso denies the proofs of God — then is God swift in reckoning.
> And if they argue with thee, then say thou: "I have submitted my face to God, as have those who follow me." And say thou to those given the Writ and to the unschooled: "Have you submitted?" And if they have submitted, then are they guided; but if they turn away, then upon thee is only the notification; and God sees the servants.
> (3:19-20)

> Is it then other than the doctrine of God they seek, when to Him has submitted whoso is in the heavens and the earth, willingly or unwillingly, and to Him they will be returned?
> Say thou: "We believe in God, and what has been sent down upon us, and what was sent down upon Abraham and

Ishmael and Isaac, and Jacob and the Grandsons; and
what was given to Moses and Jesus and the prophets
from their Lord. We make no division between any of
them, and to Him we are submitting."

And whoso seeks a doctrine other than submission, it will
not be accepted from him; and he in the Hereafter will
be among the losers.

(3:83-85)

Our Natural Instinct: Monotheism

So set thou thy face towards the doctrine, inclining to
truth: — the nature of God with which He created people — (there is no changing the creation of God) that is
the right doctrine, (but most men know not)

Turning in repentance to Him. And be in prudent fear of
Him, and uphold the duty; and be not of the idolaters:

Of those who divide their doctrine and become sects, each
party exulting at what it has.

(30:30-32)

O mankind: you are in need of God; and God, He is the
Free from Need, the Praiseworthy.

(35:15)

Prophet Abraham exemplifies the ideal of a man who put his trust
in God alone. He turned away from all idols, real and abstract, and
worshipped and implored God alone.

And who is averse to the creed of Abraham save he who
befools himself? And We chose him in the World; and
in the Hereafter he is among the righteous.

When his Lord said to him: "Submit thou," he said: "I have
submitted to the Lord of All Creation."

The same did Abraham enjoin upon his sons, as did Jacob:
"O my sons: God has chosen the doctrine for you; so die
not save when you are submitting."

If you were witnesses when death was present with Jacob:
 — when he said to his sons: "What will you serve after
 me?" — they said: "We will serve thy God, and God of
 thy fathers Abraham and Ishmael and Isaac, One God,
 and to Him are we submitting."
 (2:130-133)

Say thou: "As for me, my Lord has guided me to a straight
 path, a right doctrine, the creed of Abraham, inclining
 to truth; and he was not of the idolaters."
Say thou: "My duty and my penance and my living and my
 dying are for God, the Lord of All Creation.
"He has no partner, and that have I been commanded; and
 I am the first of those submitting."
Say thou: "Is it other than God I should desire as Lord
 when He is Lord of all things?" And every soul earns
 not save for itself, and no bearer bears the burden of
 another; then to your Lord is your return, and He will
 inform you of that wherein you differed.
 (6:161-164)

And God said: "Take not two gods. He is but One God; and
 Me — be you in fear of Me."
And to Him belongs what is in the heavens and the earth,
 and His is the doctrine forever. Will you then be in prudent fear of other than God?
 (16:51-52)

And who is better in doctrine than he who submits his
 face to God, and is a doer of good, and follows the creed
 of Abraham, inclining to truth? And God took Abraham
 as a friend.
 (4:125)

Abraham Seeks God

Prophet Abraham's journey to God is detailed in many instances in the Qur'an. He was a man of insight who did not hesitate to question his ancestral beliefs. He stood up against the majority and questioned the dominant polytheistic cult of his day. There is no mention in the Qur'an of Abraham starting a religion or cult.

> And if thou obey most of those upon the earth, they will lead thee astray from the path of God; they follow only assumption, and they are only guessing.
> (6:116)

> Abraham was neither one who holds to Judaism, nor a Christian, but was inclining to truth as one submitting; and he was not of the idolaters.
> (3:67)

> And when Abraham said to his father Āzar: "Takest thou idols as gods? I see thee and thy people in manifest error."
> And thus We showed Abraham the kingdom of the heavens and the earth; and that he might be of those who are certain.
> Then when the night covered him, he saw a star. He said: "This is my Lord." Then when it set he said: "I love not those that set."
> Then when he saw the moon rising he said: "This is my Lord." Then when it set he said: "If my Lord guide me not, I will be of the people who stray."
> Then when he saw the sun rising he said: "This is my Lord; this is greater!" Then when it set he said: "O my people: I am quit of that to which you ascribe a partnership.
> "I have turned my face towards Him who created the heavens and the earth, inclining to truth; and I am not of the idolaters."
> (6:74-79)

We are told by the leaders of every religion that the path to salvation lies in following the specific rituals, dogmas and practices of their particular religion. Men, usually, live and die in their ancestral religion.

It is only the sincere few who seek the truth.

> And when it is said to them: "Follow what God has sent
> down," they say: "Nay, we will follow that upon which
> we found our fathers," — even though their fathers did
> not reason, nor were they guided?
> (2:170)

> And when it is said to them: "Come to what God has sent
> down, and to the Messenger," they say: "Sufficient for us
> is that upon which we found our fathers." Even though
> their fathers knew not anything and were not guided?
> (5:104)

> They found their fathers astray,
> And in their footsteps are they hastening.
> (37:69-70)

Prophet Abraham correctly realized that everything created is transitory and ephemeral. Only God — the Creator — is Eternal. Thus the only logical action is to submit to the Creator alone.

> When his Lord said to him: "Submit thou," he said: "I have
> submitted to the Lord of All Creation."
> (2:131)

The religion of Islam requires that a convert recite a declaration of faith — the *shahadah* — which is not found in the Qur'an. Similarly, the Christian religion requires baptism as an integral part of its induction rites. However, Abraham — the patriarch of both religions — simply said, "I have submitted to the Lord of All Creation."

Tenets of the true faith

Time and again, God sent his messengers to re-establish His covenant with the followers of His earlier revelations who had, over time, divided themselves into various religions and sects. The messengers' mission was to call them, along with the rest of mankind, to the true faith, absent any sectarianism.

> Those who ignore warning among the doctors of the Law and the idolaters were not to desist[9] until the clear evidence came to them:
> A messenger from God, reciting purified pages[10]
> In which are upright writs.
> And those given the Writ were divided only after the clear evidence had come to them.[11]
> And they were commanded only to serve God, sincere to Him in doctrine, inclining to truth; and to uphold the duty, and to render the purity — and that is the doctrine of the upright.
> (98:1-5)

The last messenger, Muhammad, was sent to all of mankind to call them to the true faith. Those who heeded Muhammad's call joined a single unified community. However, as time went on, they, again, became divided due to mutual jealousy.[12] This is the current state of the custodians of God's last scripture; the Qur'an.

The true faith has nothing to do with following the complicated and contradictory rules and rituals found in all religions; God commands us to believe in Him and His angels, His Laws, His Messengers, and the Last Day. He admonishes us to serve and fear Him alone, and to obey His commandments exclusively.

> O you who heed warning: believe in God and His messenger and the Writ that He has sent down upon His messenger, and the Writ that He sent down before; and whoso denies God and His angels, and His Writs, and

---

9 i.e. detach from their respective religions; Judaism and Christianity (which makes Jesus a partner with God).

10 Prophet Muhammad was sent to reestablish God's covenant with the Jews and the Christians.

11 Those who received the Law would break off into sects time after time.

12 See 3:19 and 4:88.

His messengers, and the Last Day: he has strayed far away. (4:136)

(Those who heed warning, and those who hold to Judaism, and the Christians, and the Sabaeans — whoso believes in God and the Last Day and works righteousness — they have their reward with their Lord, and no fear will be upon them, nor will they grieve.)
(2:62)

If you deny — God is free from need of you. And He is not pleased, for His servants, with denial. And if you are grateful, He is pleased therewith for you. And no bearer bears the burden of another; then to your Lord is your return, and He will inform you of what you did; He knows what is in the breasts.
(39:7)

8
MAKING PARTNERS WITH GOD

There is no compulsion in doctrine; sound judgment has
become clear from error. So whoso denies idols and
believes in God, he has grasped the most firm handhold
which has no break; and God is hearing and knowing.
(2:256)

And whoso submits his face to God, and is a doer of good,
he has grasped the most firm handhold; and to God is
the final outcome of matters.
(31:22)

God does not forgive the making of partners with Him. Considering
the gravity of this sin, we must be clear on what the Qur'an means by
making a partner – or partners – with God.

God forgives not that a partnership be ascribed to Him; but
He forgives other than that whom He wills. And whoso
ascribes a partnership to God, he has strayed far away.
(4:116)

They have denied who say: "God is the Messiah, son of
Mary." And the Messiah said: "O children of Israel: serve

God, my Lord and your Lord; whoso ascribes a partnership to God, him has God forbidden the Garden, and his
shelter is the Fire; and for the wrongdoers there are no
helpers."
They have denied who say: "God is the third of three." And
there is no god save One God. And if they desist not from
so saying, there will touch those who ignore warning
among them a painful punishment.
(5:72-73)

Is then He who creates like one who creates not? Will you
then not take heed!
(16:17)

Say thou: "Who is the Lord of the heavens and the earth?"
Say thou: "God." Say thou: "Have you then taken, besides
Him, allies which have not power to do themselves
benefit or harm?" Say thou: "Is the blind equal to the
seeing? Or is darkness equal to the light?" If they have
ascribed to God partners that created the like of His
creation, then the creation appears the same to them.
Say thou: "God is creator of all things, and He is the One,
the Vanquishing."
(13:16)

Those who ignore warning will be called: "The hatred of
God is greater than your hatred of yourselves — when
you were invited to faith, but denied."
(They will say: "Our Lord: twice hast Thou given us death,
and twice hast Thou given us life; and we have confessed
our transgressions — is there to a way out any path?")
"That is because, when God was called to alone, you denied;
but if a partnership was ascribed to Him, you believed";
then judgment belongs to God, the Exalted, the Great.
(40:10-12)

On a superficial level, making a partner[13] with God means to associate a deity[14] with Him. However on a deeper level, making a partner with God means to place one's trust in anything else besides God. Those who make partners with God place their trust in their partners. They believe that their partners have the power to benefit or harm them, and trust them to come to their aid in a crisis. A believer, on the other hand, understands that only God has the power to benefit or harm him and, unlike the makers of partners, places his trust solely in God. Armed with this insight, we can see why most men are makers of partners with God, though they claim otherwise.

> And most of them believe not in God save as idolaters.
> (12:106)

> Say thou: "Travel in the earth and see how was the final outcome of those who were before; most of them were idolaters."
> So set thou thy face towards the right doctrine before there comes a day — of which there is no repelling — from God; that day will they be separated.
> (30:42-43)

When a calamity strikes, man usually calls to God for help but when God delivers him, he credits his own "smarts", Luck,[15] or other men for his deliverance.

> Then when they embark on the ship, they call to God, sincere to Him in doctrine; but when He delivers them to the land, then they ascribe a partnership,
> That they might deny what We gave them, and enjoy themselves. But they will come to know!
> (29:65-66)

---

13 or partners.
14 or deities.
15 Lady Luck. The Roman goddess of fortune; Fortuna.

He it is that created you from a single soul; and He created
therefrom its mate, that he might be reassured thereby.
Then when he covers her, she bears a light load, and she
passes by with it. And when it becomes heavy they call
to God, their Lord: "If Thou givest us a sound one, we
will be among the grateful."
Then when He gives them a sound one, they appoint Him
partners in what He gave them; but exalted is God above
that to which they ascribe a partnership!
Ascribe they a partnership to what creates not anything,
when they are created?
And they are not able to help them, nor do they help
themselves.

(7:189-192)

And when affliction touches men, they call to their Lord,
turning in repentance to Him; then when He lets them
taste mercy from Him, then a faction among them
ascribes a partnership to their Lord,
That they might deny what We have given them. So enjoy
yourselves; and you will come to know!

(30:33-34)

The Qur'an gives us specific characteristics of those who make
partners with God; after all, it is not what a man claims, but his actions,
that define him.

Separating from the true faith

The true faith — surrender to God — is an altogether different concept
from the polluted, corrupted and compromised man-made religions
masquerading as guidance from God. In reality, religions are setup by
rulers to oppress the masses. The followers of a religion are duped
into performing useless rituals, and following the dictates of priests,
rabbis and *imams* – most of whom are corrupt.

O you who heed warning: many among the rabbis and the
religious scholars consume the wealth of men in vanity,
and turn away from the path of God. And those who
amass gold and silver and spend it not in the cause of
God: give thou them tidings of a painful punishment: —
The day it will be heated in the fire of Gehenna, then
therewith will be branded their foreheads and their
sides and their backs: "This is what you amassed for
your souls; so taste what you amassed!"
(9:34-35)

Throughout history, tyrants have used religions to control the
masses by encouraging passivity and group-think, and discouraging
independent action and personal responsibility. In contrast, the true
faith frees a believer from the oppression of religion and emboldens
him to take action against his true enemies.

Those who have divided their doctrine and become sects:
thou art not of them in anything; their affair is but with
God; then will He inform them of what they did.
Whoso brings a good deed, he has tenfold the like thereof;
and whoso brings evil, he is not rewarded save with the
like thereof; and they will not be wronged.
(6:159-160)

"O you Messengers: eat of the good things, and work
righteousness; I know what you do."
And this, your community, is one community, and I am
your Lord; so be in prudent fear of Me.
But they divided their command among them into writings,
each party exulting at what it has,
So leave thou them in their flood of ignorance for a time.
(23:51-54)

The Jews, Christians and Muslims all claim to be following Prophet
Abraham — their common patriarch. The Qur'an points out that Abraham was neither a Jew nor a Christian — and by extension, nor was he

a *Muslim*;[16] he was simply one who surrendered to God.

> And they say: "Be such as hold to Judaism, or Christians
> — you will be guided." Say thou: "Nay, the creed of Abra-
> ham, inclining to truth; and he was not of the idolaters."
> Say: "We believe in God, and what has been sent down to
> us, and what was sent down to Abraham and Ishmael
> and Isaac, and Jacob and the Grandsons, and what was
> given to Moses and Jesus, and what was given to the
> prophets from their Lord; We make no division between
> any of them, and to Him are we submitting."
> Then if they believe in the like of that in which you believe,
> they have been guided; but if they turn away, they are
> only in schism. And God will suffice thee against them;
> and He is the Hearing, the Knowing.
> (2:135-137)

Abraham was neither Jew, Christian or Muslim

God also makes a conclusive argument refuting the claim that Prophet Abraham was a Christian or a Jew — or the adherent of a particular sect — since he was unaware of the implementation details of both religions.

> Say thou: "O doctors of the Law: come to an equitable
> word between us and you: that we serve not save God;
> and that we ascribe not partnership to Him; and that
> none of us takes others as lords instead of God." And
> if they turn away, then say you: "Bear witness that we
> are submitting."
> O doctors of the Law: why dispute you about Abraham,
> when the Torah and the Gospel were sent down only
> after him? Will you then not use reason!
> Here you are: those who have disputed about that whereof
> you have knowledge; why then dispute you about that

---

16 I am indebted to Brother Gerrans for this insight.

whereof you have no knowledge? And God knows, and
you know not.
Abraham was neither one who holds to Judaism, nor a
Christian, but was inclining to truth as one submitting;
and he was not of the idolaters.
The people closest to Abraham are those who have followed him, as have this prophet and those who heed
warning; and God is the ally of the believers.
(3:64-68)

During Abraham's time, the Torah and Gospel, and the Qur'an, had
not been revealed, so how could he be aware of the implementation
details of any of these religions? Even if we ignore the fact that the
doctrinal pillars of these religions are derived from sources other than
their respective Scriptures, how could Abraham — who had not studied
these Scriptures — implement the commandments and rites peculiar
to each religion? But Abraham did surrender to the Lord of all Being.
Thus anyone who wishes to follow Abraham needs only to surrender
to God; the essence of the true faith.

So set thou thy face towards the doctrine, inclining to
truth: — the nature of God with which He created people — (there is no changing the creation of God) that is
the right doctrine, (but most men know not)
Turning in repentance to Him. And be in prudent fear of
Him, and uphold the duty; and be not of the idolaters:
Of those who divide their doctrine and become sects, each
party exulting at what it has.
(30:30-32)

The fact of the matter is that the followers of the religions of Christianity, Judaism and Islam have all separated from the true faith, "each
party exulting at what it has." Those who break off from the true faith
and setup their own religions, sects or creeds are those who *make
partners with God*; they haven chosen to follow the guidance of others
— their ancestors, their favorite scholars of religion, or their own vain
desires — in preference to God's guidance.

And when it is said to them, "Follow what God has sent down," they say, "Rather, we shall follow that upon which we found our forefathers." What? Even though Satan was calling them to the blazing punishment?

(31:21)

He has ordained for you of faith what He enjoined upon Noah, and that We have inspired to you, and what We enjoined upon Abraham, Moses and Jesus that you set upright the faith and be not divided therein. Difficult for the makers of partners is what you call them towards. God chooses for Himself whoever He wills, and guides to Himself whoever turns.

And they did not split until after knowledge had come to them, out of mutual jealousy. And had it not been for a preceding Word from your Lord until a stated term, it would have been decided between them. And those who inherited the Book after them, they are uncertain of it, in doubt.

(42:13-14)

The argument God gave to Abraham

And when Abraham said to his father Āzar: "Takest thou idols as gods? I see thee and thy people in manifest error."

And thus We showed Abraham the kingdom of the heavens and the earth; and that he might be of those who are certain.

Then when the night covered him, he saw a star. He said: "This is my Lord." Then when it set he said: "I love not those that set."

Then when he saw the moon rising he said: "This is my Lord." Then when it set he said: "If my Lord guide me not, I will be of the people who stray."

Then when he saw the sun rising he said: "This is my Lord; this is greater!" Then when it set he said: "O my people: I am quit of that to which you ascribe a partnership.

> "I have turned my face towards Him who created the heavens and the earth, inclining to truth; and I am not of the idolaters."
>
> And his people disputed with him. He said: "Dispute you with me concerning God, when He has guided me? And I fear not that to which you ascribe a partnership, save that my Lord should will anything. My Lord encompasses all things in knowledge. Will you then not take heed!
>
> "And how should I fear that to which you ascribe a partnership when you fear not that you ascribe a partnership with God to that for which He has not sent down upon you authority? Then which of the two factions is worthier of security, if you know?
>
> "Those who heed warning and clothe not their faith in injustice: those have security, and they are guided."
>
> And that is Our argument We gave to Abraham against his people. We raise in degree whom We will; thy Lord is wise and knowing.
>
> (6:74-83)

The argument given by God to Abraham in defense of his monotheism was that he had no reason to fear their claimed partners of God because those who invented this lie did not fear the wrath of God, the Almighty. Hence, we come to the care of *making a partner with God*: fearing anything besides God. Cast a look around you, can you sincerely state that most of those who claim to believe in God are not *makers of partners*? Do they fear God alone? Most men — whether they call themselves Jews, Christians or Muslims — live their lives in fear of other more powerful men. They acquiesce to the wrongful orders of authority figures or the government fearing the loss of livelihood, wealth and privilege.

Trusting in wealth and children

It is natural for man to seek wealth and children as they are natural sources of enjoyment and content. However, God, the Wise, exhorts us to beware of them, as they are a trail. We must trust and rely solely upon God. Satan partners with man through his wealth and children giving him the false hope that they can help and protect him. The truth is that only God is our Ally and Protector.

> Everyone on it is to perish,
> But the face of thy Lord will remain, Owner of Majesty
> and Honour.
> (55:26-27)

> And when We said to the angels: "Submit to Adam," then
> they submitted. Not so Iblīs; he said: "Shall I submit to
> one Thou hast created of clay?"
> He said: "Hast Thou seen this whom Thou hast honoured
> above me? If Thou grant me respite until the Day of
> Resurrection, I will master his progeny save a few."
> Said He: "Depart thou! And whoso follows thee of them:
> Gehenna will be your reward; an ample reward.
> "And incite thou whom thou canst of them with thy voice,
> and rally thou horse and foot against them, and partner
> thou them in their wealth and children, and promise thou
> them," — but the satan promises them only delusion —
> "My servants: over them thou hast no authority." And thy
> Lord suffices as disposer of affairs:
> (17:61-65)

> And strike thou for them a similitude: — two men: We
> made for one of them two gardens of grapevines, and
> surrounded them with date-palms, and placed between
> them crops.
> Each of the two gardens produced its fruit and were
> wronged nothing thereof. And We caused to flow in
> the midst of them a river.
> And he had fruit, and said to his companion while con-
> versing with him: "I am greater than thee in wealth and
> mightier in men."
> And he entered his garden while he was wronging his soul,
> saying: "I think not that this will ever perish;

"And I think not that the Hour will strike; and if I am brought back to my Lord, I will find better than this as a final destination."

His companion said to him while conversing with him: "Deniest thou Him who created thee from dust; then from a sperm-drop; then fashioned thee a man?

"But as for me: He is God, my Lord, and I ascribe not a partnership with my Lord to anyone.

"And oh, that when thou wast entering thy garden thou hadst but said: 'What God has willed; there is no strength save in God!' Although thou seest me less than thee in wealth and children,

"It may be that my Lord will give me better than thy garden, and will send upon it a calamity from the sky, so that it becomes miry ground

"Or its water becomes sunken so that thou canst not find it."

And encompassed were his fruits; and he began to wring his hands for all that he had spent therein, but it was desolate and in ruins. And he said: "Would that I had not ascribed a partnership with my Lord to anyone!"

And he had no band to help him, besides God, and he could not help himself.

Thereupon protection belongs to God, the Truth! He is best in reward, and best in final outcome.

(18:32-44)

The man with the two gardens never claimed that God had a partner nor did he call to anyone besides God. Yet, in the end he cries out, "Would that I had not ascribed a partnership with my Lord to anyone!" Even though he did not make a partner with God, he did boast about his wealth and sons i.e. he trusted in his assets and received a humiliating schooling in the end. Thus, if a man believes that his wealth and children can protect or help him from the command of God, then he is making them a partner with Him. Protection belongs to God alone and only He is to be relied upon.

Trusting in might

Have they not travelled in the earth and seen how was
the final outcome of those before them? They were
more numerous than they, and stronger in power and
impact in the earth; but there availed them not what
they earned.

When their messengers came to them with clear signs,
they exulted at what they had of knowledge; but there
surrounded them that whereat they mocked.

And when they saw Our might, they said: "We believe
in God alone, and deny that to which we ascribed a
partnership!"

But their faith did not benefit them when they saw Our
might — the practice of God which has passed among
His servants[...] — and thereupon the false claimers of
guidance were lost.

(40:82-85)

Trusting in men

The media constantly brainwashes the masses into thinking that certain powerful and wealthy men are working tirelessly to save mankind
from the next great calamity.[17] Nothing could be further from the truth.
It is no secret that these billionaires have accumulated their wealth
on the backs of millions of exploited workers. These "philanthropists"
use deceptive charities, foundations and public-private partnerships
to implement long terms agendas which destabilize societies, destroy
sovereign nations and undermine men. Their end goal is to control all
the resources on the planet and to enslave all of mankind.

And the day We gather them all together, then will We say
to those who ascribe a partnership: "Where are your
partners that you claimed?"

Then will their means of denial be but that they will say:
"By God! Our Lord, we were not idolaters!"

---

17 The fake narratives of climate change, overpopulation and pandemics.

> See thou how they will lie against themselves; and strayed
> from them will be what they invented.
> (6:22-24)

The masses, for their part, worship these "philanthropists" and expect them to come to their aid. On the Day of Judgment, the defense of the masses would be that they were not makers of partners but the truth of the matter is that they *were* makers of partners because they believed that these men, besides God, could help them.

> And the day He calls them, then will He say: "Where are
> My partners whom you claimed?"
> Those upon whom the word has become binding will
> say: "Our Lord: these are they whom we caused to err.
> We caused them to err even as we ourselves did err.
> We declare our innocence to Thee; it was not us that
> they served."
> And it will be said: "Call your partners!" And they will call
> them, but they will not answer them; and they will see
> the punishment — had they but been guided!
> (28:62-64)

Christians claim that Jesus Christ will intercede on their behalf and Muslims claim the same for Muhammad. This claim, that someone can intercede on our behalf, is characteristic of those who make partners with God. The Qur'an informs us the extent of the intercession of Jesus and Muhammad and other figures on the Day of Judgment for their "followers".

> And when God will say: "O Jesus, son of Mary: didst thou
> say to men: 'Take me and my mother as two gods besides
> God?'" he will say: "Glory be to Thee! It was not for me
> to say that to which I had no right! If I had said it, then
> Thou wouldst have known it. Thou knowest what is in
> my soul, and I know not what is in Thy soul; Thou art
> the Knower of the Unseen Realms.

"I said not to them but what Thou commandedst me: 'Serve God, my Lord and your Lord.' And I was a witness to them while I was among them; but when Thou tookest me, Thou wast the watcher over them; and Thou art witness to all things.

"If Thou punish them, they are Thy servants; and if Thou forgive them, Thou art the Exalted in Might, the Wise.")
(5:116-118)

And the Messenger[18] will say: "O my Lord: my people took this Qur'an as a thing abandoned."
(25:30)

"And now have you come to Us alone, as We created you the first time; and you have left all that We conferred upon you behind your backs; and We see not with you your intercessors which you claimed were among you as partners; it is cut off between you, and strayed from you is what you claimed."
(6:94)

Say thou: "Have you seen to what you call besides God? Show me what they have created of the earth. If they have a partnership in the heavens: bring me a Writ from before this, or some remnant of knowledge, if you be truthful."

And who is further astray than he who calls, besides God, to such as will not respond to him until the Day of Resurrection? And they of their call are unaware;

And when mankind is gathered, they will be enemies to them and be deniers of their service.
(46:4-6)

And they serve, besides God, what neither harms them nor benefits them; and they say: "These are our intercessors

---

18 Muhammad.

with God." Say thou: "Would you inform God of what He knows not in the heavens or in the earth?" Glory be to Him! And exalted is He above that to which they ascribe a partnership!

(10:18)

And the day We gather them all together, then will We say to those who ascribe a partnership: "Your places — you and your partners!" Then We will separate them, and their partners will say: "It was not us you served.
"Sufficient is God as witness between us and you; we were, of your service, unaware."

(10:28-29)

Say thou: "Is there among your partners one that begins creation then repeats it?" Say thou: "God begins creation then repeats it; how then are you deluded?"
Say thou: "Is there among your partners one that guides to the truth?" Say thou: "God guides to the truth; is then He who guides to the truth worthier to be followed, or he who guides not save he be guided? Then what ails you? How judge you?"

(10:34-35)

Men worship power. The current oppressive system,[19] ultimately, derives its illusory power from the threat of its soldiers. The masses fear and obey their rulers and forget that "power belongs to God altogether, and that God is the Severe in Punishment." He, alone, is truly worthy of fear and worship.

And among men is he who takes as equals other than God, loving them with a love like the love for God. But those who heed warning are stronger in love for God. And had those who do wrong seen when they will see the punishment — that power belongs to God altogether, and that God is the Severe in Punishment —

---

19 I refer you to my book *Tyranny2.0* where I go into this system in much more detail.

When those who were followed will disown those who
   followed; and they will see the punishment, and the
   connections between them will be cut,
And those who followed will say: "Were we to return, we
   would disown them just as they have disowned us,"[...].
   Thus will God show them their deeds as regrets for them;
   and they will not come out of the Fire.
                    (2:165-167)

"And incite thou whom thou canst of them with thy voice,
   and rally thou horse and foot against them, and partner
   thou them in their wealth and children, and promise thou
   them," — but the satan promises them only delusion —
                    (17:64)

Trusting in Satan

And they will emerge before God all together; and the
   weak will say to those who had waxed proud: "We were
   your followers; can you avail us something against the
   punishment of God?" They will say: "Had God guided us,
   we would have guided you; it is the same for us whether
   we be distressed or patient: we have no place of refuge."
And the satan will say when the matter is concluded:
   "God promised you the promise of truth; and I promised you, but I betrayed you. And I had not over you
   any authority except to call you — and you responded
   to me; so blame not me, but blame yourselves. I cannot
   aid you, and you cannot aid me. I deny your ascribing
   to me a partnership before; the wrongdoers: for them
   is a painful punishment."
                    (14:21-22)

Taking one's own ego as god

Most men — although they claim to believe in a God or gods — live
their lives according to their desire i.e. they take their desire as a god.

We are not interested in what a man professes to believe; beliefs are revealed by actions. If a man serves his wishes and temptations then he is serving the satan. It is satan who commands us to act wrongfully; to hoard, to fornicate, to lust, to envy, etc. Our purpose in life is to strive against satan; not to obey him.

> And God said: "Take not two gods. He is but One God; and
> Me — be you in fear of Me."
> (16:51)

We live in an age of ego worship. Today's man lives only to satisfy his desire. This never ending foolish "pursuit of happiness" will never bring us the peace we so ardently desire. Contentment can only come by abandoning all idols — including the idol of self — and serving God alone.

> Hast thou then considered him who takes as his god his
> vain desire, and God sent him astray according to knowl-
> edge and sealed his hearing and his heart and set over
> his sight a covering? Then who will guide him after God?
> Will you then not take heed!
> (45:23)

God's arguments for His Oneness

> And they say: "God has taken a son." Glory be to Him! The
> truth is, to Him belongs what is in the heavens and the
> earth; all are humbly obedient to Him.
> The Originator of the Heavens and the Earth: when He
> decrees a matter, He but says to it: "Be thou," and it is.
> (2:116-117)

> They have denied who say: "God is the Messiah, son of
> Mary." Say thou: "Who would have power over God
> for anything if He wished to destroy the Messiah, son
> of Mary, and his mother and everyone upon the earth
> altogether?" And to God belongs the dominion of the

heavens and the earth and what is between them. He creates what He wills; and God is over all things powerful.
(5:17)

The Messiah, son of Mary, was but a messenger; messengers had passed away before him; and his mother was a woman of truth; they both ate food. See thou how We make plain the proofs to them; then see thou how they are deluded.
(5:75)

And they make for God partners of the domini, when He created them; and they ascribe to Him sons and daughters without knowledge. Glory be to Him! And exalted is He above what they describe!
The Originator of the Heavens and the Earth: how could He have a son when He has no companion, and He created all things? And He knows all things.
(6:100-101)

They take their rabbis and their religious scholars as lords rather than God, and the Messiah, son of Mary; and they were not commanded save to serve One God; there is no god save He. Glory be to Him above that to which they ascribe a partnership!
(9:31)

They say: "God has taken a son." Glory be to Him! He is the Free from Need; to Him belongs what is in the heavens and what is in the earth! You have no authority for this; do you ascribe to God what you know not?
(10:68)

And warn those who say: "God has taken a son."
No knowledge have they thereof, and nor had their fathers. Grave is the word that comes out of their mouths; they speak only a lie. (18:4-5)

It is not for God to take a son. Glory be to Him! When He
decrees a matter, He but says to it: "Be thou," and it is.)
(19:35)

And they say: "The Almighty has taken a son."
You have done a monstrous thing.
The heavens are nigh rent therefrom, and the earth split
open, and the mountains fallen in destruction
That they urge upon the Almighty a son
When it behoves not the Almighty to take a son;
There is none in the heavens and the earth but comes to
the Almighty as a servant.)
(19:88-93)

And they say: "The Almighty has taken a son." Glory be to
Him! But honoured servants
Precede Him not in word, but they act by His command.
(21:26-27)
God has not taken any son. And there is not with Him any
god; then would each god have taken what he created,
and some of them would have overcome others. Glory
be to God above what they describe —
(23:91)

Had God willed to take a son, He would have chosen from
what He created what He willed. Glory be to Him! He is
God, the One, the Vanquishing!
(39:4)

Say thou: "If the Almighty had a son, then would I be first
of those who serve."
Glory be to the Lord of the Heavens and the Earth, the
Lord of the Throne, above what they describe!
(43:81-82)

Say thou: "He is God, One!
"God, the Everlasting Refuge!

"He neither begets, nor is He begotten,
"Nor is there to Him any equal."
(112:1-4)

God's arguments for the falsity of partners

O mankind: serve your Lord who created you, and those
before you, that you might be in prudent fear;
Who made the earth for you a couch, and the sky a structure, and sent down from the sky water, then brought
forth thereby fruits as provision for you; so make not
equals to God when you know.
(2:21-22)

Knowest thou not that God, to Him belongs the dominion
of the heavens and the earth? And you have, besides
God, neither ally nor helper.
(2:107)

Hast thou not considered the one who disputed with
Abraham concerning his Lord because God had given
him dominion? When Abraham said: "My Lord is He
who gives life, and gives death," he said: "I give life, and
I give death." Abraham said: "God brings the sun from
the East; so bring thou it from the West." Then was the
one who ignored warning lost for words; and God guides
not the wrongdoing people.
(2:258)

If God helps you, none can defeat you; but if He forsakes
you, who is there who can help you after Him? And in
God let the believers place their trust.
(3:160)

Say thou: "Is it other than God I am to take as ally — the
Creator of the Heavens and the Earth, and who feeds
but is not fed?" Say thou: "I have been commanded to

be first among those who submit"; and: "Be thou not
among the idolaters."

(6:14)

"And how should I fear that to which you ascribe a partnership when you fear not that you ascribe a partnership with God to that for which He has not sent down
upon you authority? Then which of the two factions is
worthier of security, if you know?
"Those who heed warning and clothe not their faith in
injustice: those have security, and they are guided."
And that is Our argument We gave to Abraham against
his people. We raise in degree whom We will; thy Lord
is wise and knowing.

(6:81-83)

Ascribe they a partnership to what creates not anything,
when they are created?
And they are not able to help them, nor do they help
themselves.

(7:191-192)

"And those to whom you call other than Him are unable
to help you, nor do they help themselves."

(7:197)

And they serve, besides God, what neither harms them
nor benefits them; and they say: "These are our intercessors with God." Say thou: "Would you inform God
of what He knows not in the heavens or in the earth?"
Glory be to Him! And exalted is He above that to which
they ascribe a partnership!

(10:18)

Say thou: "Is there among your partners one that begins
creation then repeats it?" Say thou: "God begins creation
then repeats it; how then are you deluded?"

Say thou: "Is there among your partners one that guides
to the truth?" Say thou: "God guides to the truth; is then
He who guides to the truth worthier to be followed, or
he who guides not save he be guided? Then what ails
you? How judge you?"
(10:34-35)

In truth, to God belongs whoso is in the heavens and
whoso is in the earth; and they follow — those who call
to partners other than God — they follow only assumption; and they are only guessing.
(10:66)

And most of them believe not in God save as idolaters.
(12:106)

Say thou: "Who is the Lord of the heavens and the earth?"
Say thou: "God." Say thou: "Have you then taken, besides
Him, allies which have not power to do themselves
benefit or harm?" Say thou: "Is the blind equal to the
seeing? Or is darkness equal to the light?" If they have
ascribed to God partners that created the like of His
creation, then the creation appears the same to them.
Say thou: "God is creator of all things, and He is the One,
the Vanquishing."
(13:16)

Is then He who stands over every soul for what it earns[...]?
But they have made for God partners. Say thou: "Name
them: — if you would inform Him of what He knows not
in the earth; or if it is a show of speaking." The truth is:
their scheme has been made fair to those who ignore
warning, and they have been turned away from the path;
and whom God sends astray, for him there is no guide;
(13:33)

And those to whom they call, besides God, create not
anything, but they are created:

Dead, not living; and they perceive not when they will
be raised.

(16:20-21)

And whatever you have of favour, it is from God; then
when affliction touches you, then to Him do you cry out.

Then when He has removed the affliction from you, then a
faction among you ascribes a partnership to their Lord,

That they might deny what We have given them. So enjoy
yourselves — and you will come to know.

And they assign to what they know not a portion of what
We have provided them. By God, you will be questioned
about what you invented!

And they appoint for God daughters — glory be to Him!
— but they have what they desire;

And when one of them receives tidings of a female, his
face darkens and he suppresses grief.

He hides himself from the people because of the evil of
that whereof he had tidings — whether to hold it in
contempt, or bury it in the dust. In truth, evil is what
they judge.

For those who believe not in the Hereafter is the likeness
of evil. And for God is the highest likeness; and He is the
Exalted in Might, the Wise.

And they assign to God what they dislike

And their tongues describe the lie that for them is the best.

And were God to take men to task for their injustice, He
would not leave upon it any creature; but He delays them
to a stated term. And when their term comes, they will
not defer an hour, nor will they advance.

And they assign to God what they dislike; and their tongues
describe the lie that they will have the best. Without
doubt, they will have the Fire, and they will be rushed in.

(16:53-62)

And serve rather than God what possesses no provision
for them among the heavens or the earth at all, and can
do nothing?
(16:73)

Say thou: "If there had been gods with Him, as they say,
then would they have sought a path against the Lord
of the Throne."
(17:42)

Say thou: "Call to those whom you claim besides Him —
they have no power over the removal of affliction from
you, or of alteration."
Those to whom they call seek the means of approach to
their Lord, which of them should be nearest, and hope
for His mercy and fear His punishment; the punishment
of thy Lord is to be feared.
(17:56-57)

Your Lord is who drives for you the ships upon the sea, that
you might seek of His bounty; He is merciful towards you.
But when affliction touches you upon the sea, strayed have
those to whom you call save He. Then when He delivers
you to the land, you turn away; and man is ungrateful.
Do you feel secure that He will not cause a portion of
the land to swallow you, or send against you a storm
of stones? Then would you not find for you a guardian.
Or do you feel secure that He would not return you to it
a second time, and send against you a raging storm of
wind, and drown you for what you denied? Then would
you not find for you against Us an adherent.
(17:66-69)

And remember thou in the Writ Abraham: — he was a
man of truth and a prophet.

When he said to his father: "O my father: why servest
thou what neither hears nor sees, nor can avail thee
anything?"

"O my father: there has come to me knowledge that has
come not to thee, so follow thou me; I will lead thee to
an even path."

(19:41-43)

If they have taken gods from the earth who resurrect:

Were there in them gods save God, they would have been
corrupted; and glory be to God, the Lord of the Throne,
above what they describe!

He is not questioned about what He does, but they will
be questioned.

If they have taken gods besides Him, say thou: "Bring your
evidence. This is the remembrance of him with me, and
the remembrance of him before me." But most of them
know not the truth, so they are turning away.

(21:21-24)

And they serve, besides God, that for which He has not
sent down authority, and that whereof they have no
knowledge; and for the wrongdoers there is no helper.

And when Our proofs are recited to them as clear signs,
thou recognisest perversity in the faces of those who
ignore warning; they all but attack those who recite
Our proofs to them. Say thou: "Then shall I inform you
of worse than that? The Fire God has promised to those
who ignore warning! And evil is the journey's end."

O mankind: a similitude is struck, so listen to it: — those
to whom you call, besides God, will never create a fly
though they gather together for it. And if the fly snatch
away something from them, they could not recover it
from it; weak are the seeker and the sought!

(22:71-73)

And whoso calls, with God, to another god, whereof he
has no evidence, then is his reckoning but with his Lord;
the false claimers of guidance will not be successful.
(23:117)

And they have taken, besides Him, gods which create
nothing, but are created, and possess for themselves
neither harm nor benefit; and they possess neither
death nor life nor resurrection.
(25:3)

And they serve, besides God, what neither benefits them
nor harms them; and the false claimer of guidance is a
helper against his Lord.
(25:55)

Say thou: "Praise belongs to God, and peace be upon His
servants whom He has chosen!" Is God better, or that
to which they ascribe a partnership?
If: He who created the heavens and the earth: — and sent
down for you water from the sky wherewith We cause
to grow gardens full of delight whereof it was not for
you to cause the trees to grow — is there any god with
God? The truth is, they are a people who ascribe equals.
If: He who made the earth a fixed lodging, and made rivers
in its midst, and made firm mountains therein, and made
a barrier between the two seas: is there any god with
God? The truth is, most of them know not.
If: He who responds to one distressed when he calls to
Him, and removes the evil, and makes you successors
of the earth: is there any god with God? Little do you
take heed.
If: He who guides you in the darknesses of the land and
the sea, and who sends the winds as glad tidings at the
time of His mercy: is there any god with God? Exalted
be God above that to which they ascribe a partnership!

If: He who begins creation, then repeats it, and provides for you from the heaven and the earth: is there any god with God? Say thou: "Bring your evidence, if you be truthful." (27:59-64)

Say thou: "Have you considered: if God should make night unceasing over you until the Day of Resurrection, what god besides God will bring you illumination? Will you then not hear!"
Say thou: "Have you considered: if God should make day unceasing over you until the Day of Resurrection, what god besides God will bring you night wherein you will rest? Will you then not see!"
And of His mercy has He made for you the night and the day, that you might rest therein and seek of His bounty; and that you might be grateful. (28:71-73)

The likeness of those who take allies, besides God, is as the likeness of the spider that takes a house; and the weakest of houses is the house of the spider, did they but know. (29:41)

Then when they embark on the ship, they call to God, sincere to Him in doctrine; but when He delivers them to the land, then they ascribe a partnership,
That they might deny what We gave them, and enjoy themselves. But they will come to know! (29:65-66)

He strikes for you a similitude from yourselves: — have you from among those whom your right hands possess any partners in what We have provided for you, so that you are equal therein, you fearing them as you fear each other? Thus do We set out and detail the proofs for people who reason. (30:28)

And when affliction touches men, they call to their Lord,
turning in repentance to Him; then when He lets them
taste mercy from Him, then a faction among them
ascribes a partnership to their Lord,
That they might deny what We have given them. So enjoy
yourselves; and you will come to know!
If We have sent down upon them an authority: then it
speaks of that to which they ascribe a partnership[...].
(30:33-35)

God is He who created you; then He provided for you;
then will He give you death; then will He give you life.
Is there among your partners one who does anything
of that? Glory be to Him! And exalted is He above that
to which they ascribe a partnership!
(30:40)

"This is the creation of God; then show me what those
besides Him have created." The truth is, the wrongdoers
are in manifest error.
(31:11)

God is He who created the heavens and the earth and what
is between them in six days, then established Himself
upon the Throne. You have not, besides Him, any ally
or intercessor. Will you then not take heed!
He directs the matter from the heaven to the earth; then it
rises to Him in a day the measure whereof is a thousand
years of what you count.
That is the Knower of the Unseen and the Seen, the Exalted
in Might, the Merciful,
(32:4-6)

Say thou: "Call to those whom you claim, besides God."
They possess not the weight of an atom in the heavens or
in the earth, and they have not in them any partnership,
nor has He among them any helper. (34:22)

He makes the night enter into the day, and makes the day
enter into the night, and He made subject the sun and
the moon, each running for a stated term. That is God,
your Lord: to Him belongs the dominion; and those to
whom you call, besides Him, possess not the skin of a
date-stone.

If you call to them, they will not hear your call; and were
they to hear, they would not respond to you. And on the
Day of Resurrection they will deny your ascription of
partnership. And none can inform thee like One Aware.

(35:13-14)

Say thou: "Have you seen your partners to whom you
call instead of God? Show me what they created of the
earth!" If they have a partnership in the heavens: — or
if We have given them a Writ: — then are they upon
clear signs thereof! Nay, the wrongdoers promise one
another only delusion.

(35:40)

"And why should I not serve Him who originated me, and
to whom you will be returned?

"Shall I take gods besides Him? If the Almighty intends
me harm, their intercession will avail me nothing, nor
can they rescue me;

"Then should I be in manifest error.

(36:22-24)

But they have taken gods other than God, that they might
be helped.

They cannot help them, and they are for them a force
summoned.

(36:74-75)

And ask thou them: has thy Lord daughters and they sons?

If We created the angels females, while they were
witnesses:

(In truth, it is of their falsehood that they say:
"God has begotten," and they are liars.)
Chose He daughters over sons?
What ails you? How judge you?
Will you then not take heed!
If you have a clear authority,
Then bring your writ, if you be truthful.
(37:149-157)

God has struck a similitude: — a man concerning whom
    are partners quarrelling, and a man in submission to
    one man. Are they equal in likeness? Praise belongs to
    God! The truth is, most of them know not.
(39:29)

And if thou askest them who created the heavens and the
    earth, they will say: "God." Say thou: "Have you consid-
    ered to what you call other than God? If God wills afflic-
    tion for me, are they removers of His affliction? Or if He
    wills mercy for me, are they withholders of His mercy?"
    Say thou: "God is sufficient for me." In Him place their
    trust those who would place their trust aright.
(39:38)

And when affliction touches man, he calls to Us; then when
    We confer upon him favour from Us, he says: "I have
    only been given it according to knowledge." The truth
    is, it is a means of denial, but most of them know not.
(39:49)

Say thou: "Do you deny Him who created the earth in two
    days, and make equals to Him?" That is the Lord of All
    Creation,
(41:9)

If He has taken of what He creates daughters, and chosen
    for you sons,

(But when one of them is given glad tidings of that which
he strikes for the Almighty as a similitude, his face turns
black and he suppresses grief:
"What — one brought up among ornaments and in conflict
not seen!")
And they have made the angels, who are the servants of
the Almighty, females: — did they witness their creation? Their witness will be recorded; and they will be
questioned.
(43:16-19)

Say thou: "Have you seen to what you call besides God?
Show me what they have created of the earth. If they
have a partnership in the heavens: bring me a Writ from
before this, or some remnant of knowledge, if you be
truthful."
And who is further astray than he who calls, besides God,
to such as will not respond to him until the Day of Resurrection? And they of their call are unaware;
And when mankind is gathered, they will be enemies to
them and be deniers of their service.
(46:4-6)

Oh, that there had but helped them those whom they had
taken as gods, besides God, as a means of approach! Nay,
they strayed from them; and that was their falsehood,
and what they invented.
(46:28)

If He has daughters when you have sons:
Or if thou askest of them a reward: — then are they bur-
dened by debt.
If they have the Unseen: then are they writing.
Or if they intend a plan: then are those who ignore warning
those caught in a plan.
(52:39-42)

Have you considered Al-Lāt and Al-ʿUzzā,
And Manāt the third, the other?
Have you the males, and He the females?
That then is an unjust division.
They are only names you have named, you and your
fathers, for which God sent down no authority. They
follow only assumption, and what their souls desire;
but there has come to them guidance from their Lord.
If man is to have what he desires:
Then to God belong the Latter and the Former.
(53:19-25)

And how many an angel is there in the heavens! Their
intercession avails nothing save after that God gives
leave to whom He wills and is pleased.
Those who believe not in the Hereafter name the angels
with the names of females.
But they have no knowledge thereof, they follow only
assumption; and assumption avails nothing against
the truth.
(53:26-28)

9
RELIGIONS

From time immemorial, two institutions have subjugated man: religion and state. Religion derives its power from the fear of God,[20] and state derives its power from the fear of man.[21] Our rulers understand the power of propaganda and bring it to bear to its fullest potential in diverting the masses from God's straight path.

> And those who ignore warning say: "We will never believe in this Qur'an, nor in what was before it." But if thou couldst see when the wrongdoers are brought before their Lord, refuting each other's word[...]. Those who were despised will say to those who had waxed proud: "Were it not for you, we would have been believers!"
> Those who had waxed proud will say to those who were despised: "Did we turn you away from the guidance after it had come to you? Nay, you were lawbreakers."
> And those who were despised will say to those who had waxed proud: "Nay, it was your scheme night and day, when you commanded us to deny God and make equals to Him." And they will whisper remorse when they see the punishment, and We place yokes on the necks of those who ignore warning. Will they be rewarded save for what they did?
>
> (34:31-33)

_____

20 or gods.
21 or men.

But God is the Merciful. Throughout the ages, He sent messengers with His guidance to specific communities to guide men back to His straight path. When their communities rejected them, God delivered the believers and annihilated the rest.

Unlike previous messengers, Muhammad was sent to all of mankind. By God's help, he was successful in his mission; mankind accepted the faith in crowds. The stranglehold of religion and state was weakened for a while.

> When the help of God and the victory come,
> And thou seest mankind enter the doctrine of God in
> crowds,
> Give thou glory with the praise of thy Lord, and ask thou
> forgiveness of Him; He is accepting of repentance.
> (110:1-3)

However, the rulers of his time could not suffer the reversal of their fortunes. They set at once to divert men from the Qur'an. Their concerted efforts bore fruit: men forgot the message of the Qur'an. They went back to serving their idols instead of the One True God.

Today's man worships a plethora of idols, abstract and physical. He blindly follows his desire, he is ready and willing to kill and be killed in the name of patriotism, he works for companies that directly or indirectly exploit his fellow man, he performs idolatrous rituals which he saw his ancestors performing, he takes a "vaccine" because he believes his doctor, he censors himself because of societal pressures. In short, he follows the guidance of his idols which are inviting him to the Fire. The one thing he is not willing to do is take a sincere look at himself and accept that he is completely and utterly misguided and that only God can save him.

> Is it not that God changes not the favour He bestows upon
> a people until they change what is in their souls and that
> God is hearing and knowing!
> (8:53)

Christianity

The foundation of the religion of Christianity[22] is the belief that God is One, Eternal and Transcendent having three parts: Father, Son, and the Holy Spirit (i.e. the Holy Trinity). If God is One, then how can He be divisible into three parts? If God is transcendent (He is not subject to material limitations) then how can He "beget" a mortal (a creature subject to material limitations)? If God, Jesus Christ, and the Holy Spirit are eternal then surely Jesus Christ must have always existed. Yet, Christianity admits that he was born i.e. he did not always exist. Therefore, we are forced to reject the entire foundation of Christianity as it does not stand up to the test of reason.

Islam

The foundation of the religion of Islam[23] is the belief that God is One, Eternal and Transcendent. However, Muslims follow absurd and idolatrous practices. They believe that God commanded men to circle, bow and prostrate to a stone idol (the *Kaaba*). They circumcise their sons when in fact no such command exists in the Qur'an. The truth of the matter is that Muslims do not follow the Qur'an but their ancestors.

> O you who heed warning: wine, and games of chance, and altars, and divining arrows are an abomination of the work of the satan; so avoid it, that you might be successful.
>
> (5:90)

> And if you are in doubt about what We have sent down upon Our servant, then bring a sūrah the like thereof; and call your witnesses other than God, if you be truthful. But if you do not — and you will not — then be in prudent fear of the Fire, whose fuel is men and stones, prepared for the false claimers of guidance.
>
> (2:23-24)

---

22 Certainly, exceptions exist.
23 Certainly, exceptions exist.

And when it is said to them: "Follow what God has sent
down," they say: "Nay, we will follow that upon which
we found our fathers." — Even though the satan invites
them to the punishment of the Inferno?
(31:21)

No Requirement to Follow a Religion

Whether it be Islam, Christianity or Judaism, all religions have a specific format:

1. A belief in a deity or deities. This may be one God (monotheism), many gods (polytheism), or no god (atheism).
2. A religious class which explains its complicated instructions, rules and regulations and who conduct its rituals. They claim to have access to specialized knowledge to which the masses are not privy. The religious class cannot be questioned by the masses about their interpretation of the holy texts.
3. A specific deity which requires the performance of specific rituals and sacrifices to appease it.
4. A financial tax which is levied on its followers which is used for the maintenance of religious institutions, paying the salaries of the religious class, and (sometimes) helping the needy.

The above points are clear to any thinking man. However, it might surprise you to know that the Qur'an does not contain the blueprint of a religion.

(Those who heed warning, and those who hold to Judaism,
and the Christians, and the Sabaeans — whoso believes
in God and the Last Day and works righteousness — they
have their reward with their Lord, and no fear will be
upon them, nor will they grieve.)
(2:62)

And they say: "None will enter the Garden save such as
hold to Judaism, or are Christians." Those are their

vain desires. Say thou: "Bring your evidence, if you be truthful."

Verily, whoso submits his face to God and is a doer of good, he has his reward with his Lord; and no fear will be upon them, nor will they grieve.

And the Rabbinic Jews say: "The Christians have nothing to stand upon," and the Christians say: "The Rabbinic Jews have nothing to stand upon," when they read the Writ; thus say those who know not likewise. And God will judge between them on the Day of Resurrection concerning that wherein they differed.
(2:111-113)

And never will the Rabbinic Jews be pleased with thee, nor will the Christians, until thou follow their creed; say thou: "The guidance of God, that is guidance"; and if thou follow their vain desires after the knowledge which has come to thee, thou wilt have against God neither ally nor helper.
(2:120)

Splitting mankind into sects

Rulers maintain their power via the tried and true technique of divide-and-conquer. Using propaganda and leveraging people's tribalistic nature, their rulers split up men into racial, religious, cultural and ideological factions. Man yearns to be part of a group; to be part of something bigger than himself. But by doing so, he loses his individuality and independence. A group is a dangerous animal. The price of admission to a group is the submission of an individual's reason and sanity to the group's passion and insanity. By fanning the flames of patriotism, nationalism, and religious fanaticism within a group, its leaders —who almost always serve the rulers —are able to direct the masses to further their own agenda. The masses manufacture the chains of their own enslavement.[24] Of course, the masses are kept unaware of the real agenda.

---

24 I thank Alan Watt for this insight.

All past and present movements such as feminism, liberalism, environmentalism are expressions of this divide-and-conquer technique. The masses are constantly bombarded with propaganda via television, film, and social media to fight amongst themselves, and support an agenda while being ignorant of their true and common enemy: the deviant rulers of today. They are being deceptively led to further their own enslavement. Never in history have such powerful and all-encompassing techniques of propaganda been used by tyrants to subjugate mankind. We are truly witnessing an extraordinary event. The infamous tyrant Pharaoh used a similar technique to maintain control over the population under his dominion.[25]

> We recite to thee from the report of Moses and Pharaoh
>   with the truth for people who believe.
> Pharaoh exalted himself in the earth and made its people
>   sects; a number among them he oppressed, slaughter-
>   ing their sons and sparing their women; he was of the
>   workers of corruption.
>   (28:3-4)

Naturally, tyrants at the time of the Qur'anic revelation were incensed at the exposure of their tactics by the Qur'an and they put their best minds to work in an attempt to divert men from the truths contained within it.[26]

> They want to extinguish the light of God with their mouths;
>   but God will perfect His light, though the false claimers
>   of guidance be averse.
>   (61:8)

Complicated Rules

In the Qur'an, God has given simple, consistent and clear laws for His sincere servants. Application of these moral rules lead to individual and collective righteousness and prosperity. In contrast, the complicated

25 I refer the interested reader to my book "Tyranny 2.0" where I expound on this subject further.
26 I am indebted to Sam Gerrans for this insight.

rules of religion serve no beneficial purpose for the masses. They inevitably result in the proliferation of religious scholars whose sole job is to issue edicts and clarifications on the implementation of God's supposed complicated laws.

> And they make for God, of what He creates of tilth and cattle, a portion; they say: "This is for God," — according to their claim — "and this is for our partners". And what is for their partners, it does not reach God; and what is for God, it reaches their partners. Evil is what they judge.
> (6:136)

> "Eight pairs: of sheep two and of goats two––" Say thou: "Is it the two males He has forbidden or the two females? If what the wombs of the two females contain: inform me with knowledge, if you be truthful."
> "And of camels two and of oxen two––" Say thou: "Is it the two males He has forbidden or the two females? If what the wombs of the two females contain: — or if you were witnesses when God enjoined this upon you: — then who is more unjust than he who invents a lie about God, that he might lead people astray without knowledge? God guides not the wrongdoing people."
> (6:143-144)

Doctors of the law

God accuses the *doctors of the law* of hiding the truth and clothing it in vanity. At the time of the Qur'anic revelation, this term referred to rabbis and priests but today we can also add the religious scholars of Islam into this class. The Islamic religion, like Christianity and Judaism, is bursting at the seams with every flavor of scholar touting the benefits of his sect over others. However, God is clear: the *doctors of the law* have no authority unless they hold fast to their respective revealed Scriptures.[27]

---

27 I am thankful to Sam Gerrans for these points.

Many among the doctors of the Law wish to turn you back
as atheists after your faith out of envy from their souls
after the truth has become clear to them. But pardon
and forbear until God brings His command; God is over
all things powerful.

(2:109)

A number of the doctors of the Law would love to lead
you astray; and they lead astray only themselves, and
they perceive not.
O doctors of the Law: why deny you the proofs of God,
when you are bearing witness?
O doctors of the Law: why clothe you the truth in vanity
and conceal the truth, when you know?

(3:69-71)

And among them a faction distorts the Writ with their
tongues, that you might think it from the Writ, but it is
not from the Writ. And they say: "It is from God," but it
is not from God. And they ascribe the lie to God, when
they know.

(3:78)

Say thou: "O doctors of the Law: why turn you away from
the path of God him who believes, seeking its deviation
when you are witnesses? And God is not unmindful of
what you do."

(3:99)

O doctors of the Law: Our messenger has come to you,
making clear to you much of what you hid of the Writ,
and pardoning much. There has come to you light from
God, and a clear Writ

(5:15)

Say thou: "O doctors of the Law: you have nothing to stand
upon until you uphold the Torah and the Gospel and

what was sent down to you from your Lord." And there
increases many of them in inordinacy and denial what
was sent down to thee from thy Lord; so grieve thou
not over the people of the false claimers of guidance.
(5:68)

O you who heed warning: many among the rabbis and the
religious scholars consume the wealth of men in vanity,
and turn away from the path of God. And those who
amass gold and silver and spend it not in the cause of
God: give thou them tidings of a painful punishment: —
(9:34)

A priest uses bits of Latin while an *imam* uses Arabic catchphrases
in his sermon to an English audience. Why do these doctors of the law
not speak plainly? There are two reasons for this: First, they want to
impress their listeners with their command of a *holy* language. Second,
by using these foreign words, they become the interpreters of their
meaning. This is very important. A doctor of the law uses the layman's
ignorance of the meanings of keyterms in God's Scripture to hoodwink
him into accepting his invented rituals and doctrines.

And thus have We appointed for every prophet an enemy
— satans of servi and domini — instructing one another
in the decoration of speech as delusion, (and had thy
Lord willed, they would not have done it; so leave thou
them and what they fabricate)
And that the hearts of those who believe not in the Hereafter might incline thereto, and be pleased therewith,
and that they might commit what they are committing.
"Is it other than God I should seek as judge when He it is
that sent down to you the Writ set out and detailed?"
And those to whom We gave the Writ know that it is
sent down from thy Lord with the truth; so be thou not
of those who doubt.
(6:112-114)

Most of what these religious scholars speak is falsehood. A believing man would do well to avoid them entirely. Telling the truth to the masses is of no benefit to them. If men were told that God has sent down a clear, complete and fully detailed book containing the totality of guidance which needs to be sincerely read, pondered upon and applied by all men — regardless of their intellectual level —then these scholars would be out of business. The *imams*, priests and rabbis need people to believe that God's scripture is inscrutable and difficult to comprehend and that they alone hold the keys to its secrets.

> O you who heed warning: be in prudent fear of God, and
> believe in His messenger; He will give you a double share
> of His mercy, and appoint for you a light whereby you
> will walk, and will forgive you, — and God is forgiving
> and merciful —
> That the doctors of the Law might know that they have
> no power over the bounty of God, and that bounty is in
> the hand of God; He gives it to whom He wills; and God
> is possessor of tremendous bounty.
> (57:28-29)

Those in power do not take kindly to men bringing the truth and dismantling the false premises of their invented religions. It is high time that we see religions for what they are: a means to divide, conquer, and rule mankind.

10
THE RELIGION OF ISLAM

The religion of Islam, for all intents and purposes, is based on the *hadith* literature. These alleged sayings of the Prophet Muhammad form the backbone of the doctrinal pillars and the rituals of the religion of Islam. This should not come as a surprise as Muhammad's own people took the Qur'an in mockery.

> And the Messenger[28] will say: "O my Lord: my people took
>   this Qur'an as a thing abandoned."
>   (25:30)

The majority of Muslims have no idea what the Qur'an says; they are simply blindly following their ancestors. The Qur'an contains a stark warning in this regard.

> Then will their return be to Hell.
> They found their fathers astray,
> And in their footsteps are they hastening.
>   (37:68-70)

---

28 Muhammad.

The fact of the matter is that Muslims take the *hadith*[29] literature as the foundation of their religion. They claim that the *hadith* literature is needed to explain the Qur'an — which is quite unusual since the Qur'an itself claims to be an explanation.

> There is in their story a lesson for men of understanding;
>   it is not an invented narrative but a confirmation of
>   what is before it, and an exposition of every thing, and
>   guidance, and a mercy for people who believe.
> (12:111)

By setting up the *hadith* literature in partnership with the Qur'an, Muslims, unknowingly, have set up a partnership with God; they have taken books written by men for guidance alongside the Scripture revealed by God.

> *alif lām mīm ṣād*
> A Writ sent down to thee — so let there be no distress in
>   thy heart therefrom — that thou warn thereby, and as
>   a reminder to the believers.
> Follow what has been sent down to you from your Lord,
>   and follow not allies besides Him; little do you take heed.
> (7:1-3)

> And the day We gather them all together, then will We say
>   to those who ascribe a partnership: "Where are your
>   partners that you claimed?"
> Then will their means of denial be but that they will say:
>   "By God! Our Lord, we were not idolaters!"
> See thou how they will lie against themselves; and strayed
>   from them will be what they invented.
> (6:22-24)

---

29 Or *sunnah*. The difference being that *sunnah* is what Muhammad allegedly did while *hadith* is what he allegedly said. These terms are used interchangeably to confuse the issue as Muslims, themselves, are in confusion about what they mean. For my part, I treat them as simply non-Qur'anic literature.

The veneration of a stone idol, the *Kaaba*, in the religion of Islam is another idolatrous practice. Muslims perform the *Hajj* — a pilgrimage to Mecca — where they perform pagan rituals such as circling, bowing and prostrating to the Kaaba. This is clearly idol worship. Muslims, like the Jews before them, have cast the book of God behind their backs, preferring to follow their ancestors blindly. Is it any wonder that they are being humiliated everywhere?

> The likeness of those given to bear the Torah then have borne it not, is as the likeness of a donkey bearing books: evil is the example of the people who deny the proofs of God. And God guides not the wrongdoing people.
> (62:5)

Such is the reverence of this idol that Muslims insist on praying towards it during their ritual prayer.[30] They slaughter animals in the direction of the Kaaba. They even bury their dead in the direction of this stone idol. Muslims are not alone in erecting an idol and defying God's commandments; the people of Moses did likewise.

> And the people of Moses, while he was away, took up a calf out of their ornaments — a body that lowed. Did they not consider that it spoke not to them, neither guided them to a path? They took it up, and were wrongdoers.
> (7:148)

Circumcision is another pagan practice in the religion of Islam. Muslims falsely claim that this practice was started by Prophet Abraham; a bold lie. There is no commandment to circumcise in the Qur'an. However, Satan does command his followers to disfigure the perfect creation of God.

> They call besides to Him save to females; and they call save to a rebellious satan
> Whom God cursed; and he said: "I will take of Thy servants an appointed portion";

---

30 This direction is called the *qiblah*.

And: "I will lead them astray"; and: "I will arouse desires
in them"; and: "I will command them and they will slit
the ears of cattle"; and: "I will command them and they
will change the creation of God." And whoso takes the
satan for ally instead of God, he has suffered clear loss.
He promises them, and arouses desires in them; and the
satan promises them only delusion.
He promises them, and arouses desires in them; and the
satan promises them only delusion.
(4:117-120)

Muslims claim that God requires a man to convert to the religion
Islam. However, according to the Qur'an, *islam*[31] simply means to *submit
to God*, not to convert to a specific religion. All messengers, prophets
and men of God were *muslims* because they submitted to God alone.
I must emphasize that the religion of Islam and *islam,* submission to
God, are entirely different concepts.[32] The former is a membership to a
group with its requisite rituals, dogma, and regulations. The latter is a
personal choice — taken by a man who accepts individual responsibility
for his actions — to believe in God and serve Him alone.

Nowhere in the Qur'an does God require a man who wishes to submit to Him to convert to a religion called Islam, perform a ritualistic
prayer facing the Kaaba, pay a fixed religious tax or circle a stone idol
in Mecca. Muslims justify these invented practices by turning to the
hadith, arguing that since their details are not found in the Qur'an, they
need the *hadith* literature to explain them i.e. the Qur'an is somehow
deficient.

The Qur'an is Clear, Complete, and Fully Detailed

The fact of the matter is that the Qur'an is clear, complete and fully
detailed. The reason the implementation details of many of the rituals of
the Muslims are not found in the Qur'an is because they were invented
by their predecessors and are not a part of the true faith in the Qur'an.

---

31 With a lowercase *i.*
32 I am indebted to Sam Gerrans for this insight.

A moon of scorching heat was that in which the Qur'an
was sent down, a guidance for mankind, and clear signs
of the guidance and the Division[...]. So whoso among
you witnesses the moon, let him fast in it. And whoso
of you is sick or on a journey: then a number of other
days. God desires for you ease, and He desires not for
you hardship; but that you complete the number; and
that you magnify God for guiding you; and that you
might be grateful.

(2:185)

O you who heed warning: enter into surrender completely,
and follow not the footsteps of the satan; he is to you
an open enemy.
But if you slip after the clear signs have come to you, then
know that God is exalted in might and wise.
(2:208-209)

O mankind: there has come to you evidence from your
Lord; and We have sent down to you a clear light
(4:174)

O doctors of the Law: Our messenger has come to you,
making clear to you much of what you hid of the Writ,
and pardoning much. There has come to you light from
God, and a clear Writ
Whereby God guides him who seeks His approval to the
ways of peace, and brings them out of darkness into the
light by His leave; and He guides them to a straight path.
(5:15-16)

And We sent down to thee the Writ with the truth, confirming what is before it of the Writ, and as a control
over it. So judge thou between them by what God has
sent down; and follow thou not their vain desires away
from what has come to thee of the truth. For each of you
We appointed an ordinance and a procedure. And had

God willed, He could have made you one community;
but that He might try you in what He gave you[...]. — So
vie in good deeds; unto God will you return all together,
and He will inform you of that wherein you differed —
And judge thou between them by what God has sent down;
and follow thou not their vain desires, and beware thou
of them lest they seduce thee away from some of what
God has sent down to thee. And if they turn away, know
thou that God but intends to afflict them for some of their
transgressions; and many among men are perfidious.
Is it the judgment of ignorance they seek? And who is
better than God in judgment for people who are certain?
(5:48-50)

And thus We expound the proofs: both that they might
say: "Thou hast studied," and that We might make it
plain for people who know.
(6:105)

And We have brought them a Writ which We set out and
detailed according to knowledge — a guidance and
mercy for people who believe.
(7:52)

And when Our proofs are recited to them as clear signs,
those who look not for the meeting with Us say: "Bring
thou a Qur'an other than this; or change thou it." Say
thou: "It is not for me to change it of my own accord.
I follow only what is revealed to me. I fear, if I should
disobey my Lord, the punishment of a tremendous day."
(10:15)

alif lām rā Those are the proofs of the Clear Writ.
We have sent it down as an Arabic recitation, that you
might use reason.
(12:1-2)

That is of the reports of the Unseen which We reveal to thee; and thou wast not with them when they resolved upon their affair, when they were scheming.

And most men — though thou be desirous — are not believers.

And thou askest not of them for it any reward; it is only a reminder to all mankind.

And how many a proof is there in the heavens and the earth which they pass by, and from which they turn away!

And most of them believe not in God save as idolaters.

Do they then feel secure against an enveloping of the punishment of God coming upon them, or the Hour coming upon them unexpectedly when they perceive not?

Say thou: "This is my path. I invite to God with insight — I and whoso follows me. And glory be to God! And I am not of the idolaters."

And We sent before thee only men to whom We revealed from among the people of the cities. (So have they not travelled in the earth and seen how was the final outcome of those who were before them? And the abode of the Hereafter is best for those who are in prudent fear; will you then not use reason!)

When the messengers had despaired and thought that they had been denied, there came to them Our help and who We willed was delivered. And repulsed not is Our wrath from the lawbreaking people.

There is in their story a lesson for men of understanding; it is not an invented narrative but a confirmation of what is before it, and an exposition of every thing, and guidance, and a mercy for people who believe.

(12:102-111)

This is a notification to mankind, that they be warned thereby, and that they might know that He is but One God, and that those of insight might take heed.

(14:52)

alif lām rā Those are the proofs of the Writ and of a clear
   recitation.
                              (15:1)

And the day We raise in every community a witness against
   them from themselves, and We bring thee as a witness
   against these[...]. And We sent down the Writ upon thee
   as a clarification of all things, and as guidance, and as a
   mercy, and as glad tidings for those submitting.
                              (16:89)

This Qur'an guides to what is most upright, and brings
   glad tidings to the believers who do righteous deeds,
   that they have a great reward,
And that those who believe not in the Hereafter: — We
   have prepared for them a painful punishment.
And man supplicates for evil by his supplication for good;
   and man is ever hasty.
And We appointed the night and the day as two proofs;
   and We erase the proof of the night and make the proof
   of day sight-giving, that you might seek favour of your
   Lord, and that you might know the number of years
   and the reckoning; and everything have We set out and
   detailed with full explanation.
                              (17:9-12)

And We send down of the Qur'an what is a healing and
   mercy for the believers; but it increases not the wrongdoers save in loss.
                              (17:82)

And We have expounded in this Qur'an, that they take
   heed; but it increases them only in aversion.
                              (17:41)

And We have expounded for men in this Qur'an every
   similitude, but most men refuse save denial. (17:89)

And with the truth have We sent it down, and with the
truth has it come down — and We sent thee only as a
bearer of glad tidings and a warner —
And as a recitation We divided, that thou recite it to men
in stages; and We have sent it down as a successive
revelation.
(17:105-106)

And We have expounded for men in this Qur'an every
similitude, but man is, more than anything, contentious.
(18:54)

A sūrah We have sent down and made obligatory, and
wherein We sent down clear proofs, that you might
take heed:
(24:1)

And the day the sky is rent asunder with the clouds, and
the angels are sent down in successive descent,
True dominion, that day, belongs to the Almighty; and it
will be a difficult day for the false claimers of guidance.
And the day the wrongdoer will bite his hands, he will
say: "Would that I had taken with the Messenger a path!
"Woe is me! Would that I had not taken such-and-such
for a friend!
"He led me astray from the remembrance after it reached
me." And the satan is to man a traitor.
And the Messenger will say: "O my Lord: my people took
this Qur'an as a thing abandoned."
And thus We appointed for every prophet an enemy from
among the lawbreakers; but thy Lord suffices as a guide
and a helper.
And those who ignore warning say: "Oh, that the Qur'an
were but sent down upon him all at once!" Thus — that
We might strengthen thy heart thereby; and We have
recited it distinctly.

And they bring thee not a similitude save We bring thee
the truth and better in explanation.

(25:25-33)

And thus have We appointed for every prophet an enemy
— satans of servi and domini — instructing one another
in the decoration of speech as delusion, (and had thy
Lord willed, they would not have done it; so leave thou
them and what they fabricate)
And that the hearts of those who believe not in the Hereafter might incline thereto, and be pleased therewith,
and that they might commit what they are committing.
"Is it other than God I should seek as judge when He it is
that sent down to you the Writ set out and detailed?"
And those to whom We gave the Writ know that it is
sent down from thy Lord with the truth; so be thou not
of those who doubt.
And perfected is the word of thy Lord in truth and justice; there is none to change His words; and He is the
Hearing, the Knowing.
And if thou obey most of those upon the earth, they will
lead thee astray from the path of God; they follow only
assumption, and they are only guessing.

(6:112-116)

And it is a revelation of the Lord of All Creation,
Brought down by the Faithful Spirit
Upon thy heart — that thou be of the warners —
In a clear Arabic tongue.

(26:192-195)

This Qur'an relates to the children of Israel most of that
wherein they differ,
And it is guidance, and a mercy for the believers.
Thy Lord will decide[33] between them by His judgment;
and He is the Exalted in Might, the Knowing.

---

33 Or decides.

And place thou thy trust in God; thou art upon the manifest truth.
(27:76-79)

"I have but been commanded to serve the Lord of this land
who made it inviolable;and to Him all things belong. And
I am commanded to be of those submitting,
"And to recite the Qur'an." And whoso is guided, he is but
guided for himself; and whoso strays, then say thou: "I
am only of the warners."
(27:91-92)

He who made the Qur'an incumbent upon thee will return
thee to a destination. Say thou: "My Lord best knows
who brings guidance and who is in manifest error."
And thou didst not expect that the Writ would be cast unto
thee;[...] only as a mercy from thy Lord, so be thou not
a helper to the false claimers of guidance.
And let them not turn thee away from the proofs of God
after they have been sent down to thee; and invite thou
to thy Lord, and be thou not of the idolaters.
And call thou not with God to another god; there is no god
save He. Everything will perish save His face; His is the
Judgment; and to Him will you be returned.
(28:85-88)

And We have struck for men in this Qur'an every similitude. And if thou come to them with a proof, those who
ignore warning will say: "You are only creators of vanity."
(30:58)

And had all that is in the earth of trees been but pens,
and the sea replenished thereafter with seven seas, the
words of God would not be exhausted; God is exalted
in might and wise.
(31:27)

And when Our proofs are recited to them as clear signs, they say: "This is only a man who wishes to turn you away from what your fathers served"; and they say: "This is only an invented falsehood." And those who ignore warning say of the truth when it has come to them: "This is only obvious sorcery."
(34:43)

And We taught him not poetry, and it does not behove him; it is only a remembrance and a clear recitation
To warn whoso is alive, and that the word might become binding against the false claimers of guidance.
(36:69-70)

And We have struck for mankind in this Qur'an every similitude, that they might take heed;
An Arabic recitation, free of deviation, that they might be in prudent fear.
(39:27-28)

ḥā mīm
A revelation from the Almighty, the Merciful,
A Writ the proofs whereof are set out and detailed, an Arabic recitation for people who know,
As a bearer of glad tidings and a warner; but most of them turn away, so they hear not.
(41:1-4)

ḥā mīm
By the Clear Writ!
We have made it an Arabic recitation, that you might use reason,
And it is in the foundation of the Writ, with Us, exalted and wise.
Shall We then turn the remembrance away from you because you are a people committing excess?
(43:1-5)

The Almighty:
Taught the Qur'an,
Created man,
Taught him the clear statement.
(55:1-4)

(Move thou not thy tongue with it to hasten it.
Upon Us is its gathering and its recitation.
And when We recite it, follow thou the recitation thereof.
Then upon Us is its clarification.)
(75:16-19)

He it is that sends down to His servant clear proofs, that
He might bring you out of darkness into the light; and
God is to you kind and merciful.
(57:9)

The truth is, it is a glorious recitation,
In a protected tablet.
(85:21-22)

Sects within the Religion of Islam

Like Christianity and Judaism before it, Islam has split up into numerous sects; Sunni and Shia being the two dominant ones. If Muslims claim that their religion is the perfect religion, then why have they splintered into sects? If its adherents follow the same Scripture and the same prophet then why are their differences such that they warrant a complete schism? The Qur'an gives us the answer: men split up into sects due to envy and jealousy.

Mankind was one community; then God raised up prophets as bearers of glad tidings and warners, and sent down with them the Writ with the truth, that He might judge between men concerning that wherein they differed. And there differed therein only those who were given it, after clear signs had come to them, through sectarian zealotry between them. But God guided those who heeded warning to that of the truth concerning which they differed, by His leave; and God guides whom He wills to a straight path.

(2:213)

This, your community, is one community, and I am your
Lord; so serve Me.
But they divided their affair between them; all are returning to Us.
And whoso works any righteous deeds, and is a believer:
there is no rejection of his effort, and We are writers
for him.

(21:92-94)

And they became divided only after knowledge came to them, through sectarian zealotry between them. And were it not for a word that preceded from thy Lord to a stated term, it would have been concluded between them. And those who were caused to inherit the Writ after them are in sceptical doubt concerning it.

(42:14)

The Qur'an does not condone the splitting up of believers into sects. Men differ in all sorts of trivial matters and it comes as no surprise that they would differ in such a great matter — interpreting God's holy word. However, to let differences in opinion result in a schism within our community is defying the basic teachings of the Qur'an. All believers are to hold fast to the Qur'an and not be divided therein.

And those who hold fast the Writ, and uphold the duty —
We cause not to be lost the reward of those who do right.

(7:170)

The Five Pillars of Islam

The religion of Islam is based on five doctrinal pillars. A Muslim must observe them to be considered a practicing *Muslim*.

1. *Shahadah*
2. *Salaat*
3. *Sawm*
4. *Zakat*
5. *Hajj*

Shahadah

The *shahadah*, a testification of faith, is the de-facto requirement to convert to the religion of Islam. It translates to: *there is no God but God and Muhammad is the messenger of God*. However, this *complete* statement is not found anywhere in the Qur'an.[34] To be clear I am not arguing that we are not to believe in God and His messengers but simply pointing out that this *complete* statement and the *requirement* to say it is not found in the Qur'an. How then is it possible that the Qur'an does not mention this *fundamental* requirement to become a Muslim in full? It is not possible. Therefore, those who insist that a man must utter the *shahadah* — the full text of which is not found in the Qur'an — are not following the Qur'an but outside sources.

> God bears witness that there is no god save He, as do the angels and those of knowledge upholding equity: "There is no god save He, the Exalted in Might, the Wise."
> (3:18)

God testifies that there is no God but Him; those *possessed of knowledge* testify to this as well. This, then, is the true *testimony* to which all believers are to testify to if they are to testify to anything. The Qur'an gives us example of the previous submitters to God. As you can see a *shahadah* was not uttered by any of them.

> And who is averse to the creed of Abraham save he who befools himself? And We chose him in the World; and in the Hereafter he is among the righteous.

---

34 I am indebted to Sam Gerrans for this insight.

When his Lord said to him: "Submit thou," he said: "I have
submitted to the Lord of All Creation."
(2:130-131)

And the sorcerers fell in submission.
They said: "We believe in the Lord of All Creation,
"The Lord of Moses and Aaron."
(7:120-122)

(It was said to her: "Enter thou the palace." But when she
saw it, she thought it a body of water and uncovered her
legs. He said: "It is a palace made smooth with glass.")
She said, "My Lord: I have wronged my soul, and I submit
with Solomon to God, the Lord of All Creation."
(27:44)

The *shahadah* of the religion of Islam treats Muhammad as a special
messenger — Muslims would certainly balk at the idea of replacing
Moses with Muhammad in the *shahadah*. However, the Qur'an specifically states that the believers do not make a distinction between
any of God's messengers. We must hear and obey God's imperatives
completely and sincerely if we claim to submit to Him.

The Messenger believes in what is sent down to him from
his Lord, as do the believers; each believes in God and
His angels, and His Writs and His messengers: "We
make no distinction between any of His messengers."
And they say: "We hear and we obey; Thy forgiveness
our Lord[...]. And to Thee is the journey's end."
(2:285)

Salaat

Muslims claim that God commands them to perform a ritual prayer
five times a day. In broad strokes, Muslims perform this ritual prayer
by facing the direction of the *Kaaba* in Mecca. They stand and recite
short chapters from the Qur'an in Arabic, regardless of whether they

understand them or not. After this recitation, they bow, stand, prostrate, and sit in a specific manner. Depending on the prayer time, these actions are repeated a number of times.

According to the Qur'an, *salaat* is not a ritual prayer. Even if we do entertain the possibility that it is a ritual prayer, then we encounter a further problem. The five *salaats* (*fajr, zuhr, asr, maghrib*, and *isha*) of the Islamic religion are not mentioned by name in the Qur'an. Only two[35] of these five *salaats* are mentioned by name (*fajr* and *isha*). This is an incontestable fact. However, the problems for Muslims do not end here; God commands the believers to uphold the *salaat* in many places in the Qur'an, but the details of how to perform such an important ritual are conspicuously absent therein. However, if we take a step back and look at the usage of the word *salaat* across the entire Qur'an, we realize that it is an abstract noun which simply means *duty*;[36] and while worshipping God is a believer's primary duty, there are many other duties incumbent upon him in the Qur'an.

It is precisely because of Muslims' arrogant approach to the Qur'an — justifying their inherited beliefs and practices instead of trying to understand God's word — that they misunderstand what the Qur'an means by *salaat*. They reflexively think *ritual prayer* when they read the word *salaat* in the Qur'an. When they do not find the details of this ritual prayer in the Qur'an, they revert to non-Qur'anic sources. The sincere approach to God's book is to investigate *its* usage of words and not impose our meanings of words upon it.[37]

Sawm

Sawm which means *fasting*, is another requirement of the religion of Islam. Muslims must fast throughout a special holy month called *Ramadan*. During this fast, which lasts from dawn to sunset, Muslims must abstain from eating, drinking, and sexual intercourse. It is true that fasting is stipulated in the Qur'an, but it is left up to a believer as to how many days he wishes to fast.

---

35 Or three, depending on how you classify the word *wustaa*.
36 I am indebted to Sam Gerrans for this insight.
37 See Chapter 11 for a demonstration of this technique.

O you who heed warning: fasting is prescribed for you:
— as it was prescribed for those before you, that you
might be in prudent fear —

For days numbered. And whoso among you is sick or on a
journey: then a number of other days. And for those who
are able to do it is a redemption: feeding a needy person.
And whoso does good voluntarily, it is better for him.
And that you fast is better for you, if you would know.

A moon of scorching heat was that in which the Qur'an
was sent down, a guidance for mankind, and clear signs
of the guidance and the Division[...]. So whoso among
you witnesses the moon, let him fast in it. And whoso
of you is sick or on a journey: then a number of other
days. God desires for you ease, and He desires not for
you hardship; but that you complete the number; and
that you magnify God for guiding you; and that you
might be grateful.

And when My servants ask thee concerning Me: "I am
near." I respond to the call of the caller when he calls to
Me. So let them respond to Me, and let them believe in
Me, that they might be guided.

It is made lawful for you on the night of the fast to go in
unto your women. They are a covering for you, and you
are a covering for them. God knows that you deceived
yourselves, so He turned towards you and pardoned
you; so now lie with them and seek what God has prescribed for you. And eat and drink until clear to you be
the white thread from the black thread of the dawn.
Then complete the fast until night. And lie with them
not when you remain in the places of worship. Those
are the limits of God, so approach them not. Thus does
God make plain His proofs to men, that they might be
in prudent fear.

(2:183-187)

Muslims cite the above verses to justify their practice of fasting throughout a month called *ramadan*.[38] However, the directive to fast during this month was for those who witnessed the revelation of the Qur'an during it[39] i.e. Muhammad's contemporaries. We cannot fast during *ramadan* simply because we did not witness this extraordinary event. In today's age, a believer must fast "for days numbered" i.e. according to his devotion and strength.

Zakat

According to Islam, *zakat* is a mandatory charitable contribution, often considered to be a tax. The amount is fixed at 2.5% of one's savings. This fixed percentage is found nowhere in the Qur'an. It is simply left up to the believer how much money he wants to spend in the cause of God. The primary meaning of *zakat* is *purification*. The claim that *zakat* is *an annual obligatory religious tax* is not supported by the Qur'an.

Hajj

The last pillar of the religion of Islam, called *Hajj*, is an annual pilgrimage to Mecca which, plainly speaking, is idol worship. The Qur'anic *hajj* was an altogether different concept from the idol worship being practiced in Mecca today. We look at *Hajj* in detail in the next chapter.

---

38 The timings of which are dictated by an Islamic calendar.
39 "So whoso among you witnessses the moon..." (2:185)

11
THE HAJJ RITUAL

Accordingto the religion of Islam, every Muslim adult is required to undertake the *Hajj* pilgrimage at lease once in his lifetime, if he is financially and physically able to do so. The *hajj* in the Qur'an has nothing to do with visiting Mecca and revering a stone idol. It was started by prophet Abraham to invite men to God.

> And when We settled for Abraham the position of the house: "Ascribe thou not a partnership with Me to anything; and purify thou My house for those who walk around, and those who stand, and the lowly, and the submitting.
> "And proclaim thou among mankind the pilgrimage; they will come to thee on foot, and on every lean mount; they will come from every deep mountain pass,
> "That they might witness benefits for them, and remember the name of God on days appointed over their provision of livestock cattle." So eat thereof, and feed the unfortunate poor;
> Then let them make an end of their unkemptness, and fulfil their vows, and walk around the ancient house.
> (22:26-29)

128

The word *hajj* is based on the roots *h-j-j* and the Qur'an uses words based on this root to mean *to dispute* or *to debate*.[40]

> And when they will dispute[41] together in the Fire, the weak will say to those who had waxed proud: "We were your followers; will you avail us something against a portion of the Fire?"
>
> (40:47)

> And those who dispute[42] concerning God after that answer has been made to him: their argument[43] has no weight with their Lord; and upon them is wrath, and they have a severe punishment.
>
> (42:16)

As the final messenger and prophet to all of mankind, Muhammad was commanded to re-institute the *hajj*. Prophet Muhammad and the believers were to once again sanctify the house at *the inviolable place of worship*.[44] Muslims claim that this place is in Mecca (and the Kaaba is the house), however there is strong evidence to suggest that it was elsewhere. What is important to understand is that *Hajj* of today is pure idol worship when God specifically warns us to not worship idols.

The Nabateans — the ancestors of the Arabs — worshipped idols in symbolic forms such as standing stones. They claimed that these stone idols, called *betyls,* represented their deity. [45]

---

40 2:76, 2:139, 2:150, 2:158, 2:189, 2:196, 2:197, 2:258, 3:20, 3:61, 3:65, 3:66, 3:73, 3:97, 4:165, 6:80, 6:83, 6:149, 9:3, 9:19, 22:27, 28:27, 40:47, 42:15, 42:16, 45:25.
41 Arabic: yatahajjuna.
42 Arabic: yuhajjuna.
43 Arabic: hujjatuhum.
44 Arabic: al masjid-al-haram.
45 Wenning, Robert. The Betyls of Petra. Bulletin of the American Schools of Oriental Research, 2001.

Nabataean baetyl depicting a goddess, possibly al-Uzza

The Kaaba is one such "standing stone" which was appropriated into the religion of Islam. However, the Qur'an is clear on this subject; all idols, of whatever form, are forbidden. The Qur'an uses the word *nasbun* (root *n-s-b)* to mean any *erected structure.* Lane's lexicon describes it as: "A sign, or mark, set up to show the way; or a standard set up". The Kaaba is such an erected structure towards which the Muslims prostrate during their ritual prayer.

> And We raised up in every community a messenger: "Serve God and avoid idols." And among them was he whom God guided; and among them was he upon whom misguidance was binding. So travel in the earth and see how was the final outcome of the deniers.
> (16:36)

> O you who heed warning: wine, and games of chance, and altars,[46] and divining arrows are an abomination of the work of the satan; so avoid it, that you might be successful.
> (5:90)

> The day they will come forth from the graves in haste, as though towards an idol,[47] running,
> Their eyes humbled, humiliation covering them. That is the day which they are promised.
> (70:43-44)

> And at the mountains — how they were erected![48]
> (88:19)

Pagan Religions and Circumambulation

The defining feature of the *Hajj* is the circling of the *Kaaba* idol counter-clockwise seven times. The Qur'an does not mention the circling of any object seven times. However, this practice is found in Hinduism,

46 Arabic: wa-alansaabu.
47 Arabic: nusubin.
48 Arabic: nusibat.

among other pagan religions.

> The saat phere is one of the most important features of the Hindu Wedding, involving seven rounds around a sacred fire lit for the purpose amidst the Vedic mantras. The bride and groom circumambulate a consecrated fire seven times, reciting specific vows with each circuit (Sanskrit: parikrama). Vows made in the presence of the sacred fire (Sanskrit: agni) are considered unbreakable, with Agnideva held as both witnessing and blessing the couple's union. Every phera taken holds a specific meaning. And in according to vedas [parikrama] is from origin of hindu dharma, according to vedas it is lords ritual of acceptances of soul.[49]
>
> Parikrama or Pradakshina is clockwise circumambulation of sacred entities, and the path along which this is per-formed, as practiced in the Indic religions - Hinduism, Buddhism, Sikhism and Jainism.[1][2][3][4][5] In Buddhism, it refers only to the path along which this is performed.[3] Typically, in Indic-religions the parikrama is done after completion of traditional worship (puja) and after paying homage to the deity. Parikrama must be done with dhyāna (spiritual contemplation and meditation).[50]

The Hajj ritual details

I shall now look at some of the key rituals in the Muslim *Hajj* to show you how Muslims have taken Qur'anic keywords out of context to justify their invented practices. Below is an excerpt from the article on *Hajj* on Wikipedia.

> When the pilgrims reach the appropriate Miqat (7:142, 56:50) (depending on where they have come from), they are believed to enter into a state of holiness – known as Ihram – that consists of wearing two white seamless

49 "Saat Phere." Wikipedia, 21 Jan. 2022, en.wikipedia.org/wiki/Saat_phere.
50 "Parikrama." Wikipedia, 27 Sept. 2022, en.wikipedia.org/wiki/Parikrama. Accessed 29 Oct. 2022.

cloths for the male, with the one wrapped around the waist reaching below the knee and the other draped over the left shoulder and tied at the right side;[51]

Muslims start the *Hajj* by donning a special wardrobe called the *Ihram* at any of five specific places called *Miqats*. This requirement to dress a certain way at a specific place in order to start a *hajj* is not in the Qur'an. The Qur'an uses the word *miqat* consistently[52] to mean *a time appointed*.

And We appointed for Moses thirty nights, and completed them with ten; so he completed the time appointed[53] by his Lord of forty nights. And Moses said to his brother Aaron: "Be thou my successor among my people; and make thou right; and follow thou not the path of the workers of corruption."
(7:142)

Say thou: "The former peoples and the latter
"Will be gathered together at the appointed time[54] of a known day."
(56:49-50)

Miqat, which simply means *a time appointed* in the Qur'an, was twisted to mean a point where a pilgrim puts on special clothing in preparation for the *Hajj*. It is worth nothing that the *Ihram* dress worn by Muslims pilgrims matches the style of the *Kasaya*; a special clothing worn by Buddhist monks. Continuing on with the article:

The ritual of Tawaf (52:24, 56:17, 76:19) involves walking seven times counterclockwise around the Kaaba. Upon arriving at Al-Masjid Al-Ḥarām (The Sacred Mosque), pilgrims perform an arrival tawaf either as part of Umrah or

51 Wikipedia Contributors. "Hajj." Wikipedia, Wikimedia Foundation, 13 Mar. 2019, en.wikipedia.org/wiki/Hajj.

52 2:189, 7:142, 7:143, 7:155, 26:38, 44:40, 56:50, 78:17.

53 Arabic: miqatu.

54 Arabic: miqati.

as a welcome tawaf. During tawaf, pilgrims also include Hateem – an area at the north side of the Kaaba – inside their path. Each circuit starts with the kissing or touching of the Black Stone (Hajar al- Aswad). If kissing the stone is not possible because of the crowds, they may simply point towards the stone with their hand on each circuit. Eating is not permitted but the drinking of water is allowed, because of the risk of dehydration.

According to the Qur'an, the word *ta`if* (Tawaf) means *a visitation* and not to circle something seven times. *Ta'if* is based on the root t-w-f and words based on this root occur thirty-five times[55] in the Qur'an. I invite you to go through each of them to confirm that they can only mean *a visitation*,[56] *to walk around*,[57] *a group*,[58] *flood*,[59] *mingle*[60] and *to go about*.[61] There is no instance in the Qur'an where words based on the root *t-w-f* can possibly mean *to circle the Kaaba seven times.* Below are all Qur'anic verses containing the word *ta'if*.

> And when We made the house a meeting place for mankind, and a place of security — and make from the station of Abraham a place of duty — and We made a covenant with Abraham and Ishmael: "Purify My house for those who *lil-ta`iffin*, and those who remain, and the lowly and the submitting."
>
> (2:125)

> Those who are in prudent fear, when a *ta`iffun* from the satan touches them, they take heed — and then do they see.
>
> (7:201)

---

55 2:125, 2:158, 3:69, 3:72, 3:122, 3:154, 4:81, 4:102, 4:113, 6:156, 7:87, 7:133, 7:201, 8:7, 9:66, 9:83, 9:122, 22:26, 22:29, 24:2, 24:58, 28:4, 29:14, 33:13, 37:45, 43:71, 49:9, 52:24, 55:44, 56:17, 61:14, 68:19, 73:20, 76:15, 76:19.
56 Arabic: ta'if.
57 Arabic: tatawuff.
58 Arabic: ta'ifattun.
59 Arabic: tufaan.
60 Arabic: tawwafun.
61 Arabic: tafa.

And when We settled for Abraham the position of the
house: "Ascribe thou not a partnership with Me to anything; and purify thou My house for those who *lil-ta`iffin*,
and those who stand, and the lowly, and the submitting.
(22:26)

Then an *ta`iffun* from thy Lord went about it while they
slept,
(68:19)

It would surprise you to know that Muslims believe that the footprints of Prophet Abraham are still preserved near the Kaaba; which
they call the *Maqam Ibrahim*.

The Maqām Ibrāhīm (lit. 'Station of Abraham')[1][2] is a
stone associated with Abraham, Ishmael and their
rebuilding of the Ka'bah in what is now the Great Mosque
of Mecca in Saudi Arabia. According to Islamic tradition,
the imprint on the stone came from Abraham's feet.[3][4]
According to one tradition it appeared when Abraham
stood on the stone while building the Kaaba; when the
walls became too high, Abraham stood on the maqām,
which miraculously rose up to let him continue building and also miraculously went down in order to allow
Ishmael to hand him stones. Other traditions held that
the footprint appeared when the wife of Ishmael washed
Abraham's head, or alternatively when Abraham stood
atop it in order to summon the people to perform the
pilgrimage to Makkah .[62]

This term *maqam ibrahim* – which we are to believe is a set of
footprints left by Abraham – is mentioned in the Qur'an, but it means
something else entirely. Again, we encounter the tactic of twisting
a general term to assign it a special cultic significance. The *maqam
ibrahim* in the Qur'an is not a set of footprints but the original duty of

62 "Maqam Ibrahim." Wikipedia, 25 July 2022, en.wikipedia.org/wiki/Maqam_Ibrahim.
Accessed 29 Oct. 2022.

Abraham to initiate the *Hajj*; God commanded prophet Muhammad to do likewise; to follow in Abraham's footsteps.

> And when his Lord tried Abraham with words and he fulfilled them, He said: "I will make thee a leader for mankind." Said he: "And of my progeny?" He said: "My covenant does not reach the wrongdoers."
>
> And when We made the house a meeting place for mankind, and a place of security — and make from the station of Abraham[63] a place of duty — and We made a covenant with Abraham and Ishmael: "Purify My house for those who walk around, and those who remain, and the lowly and the submitting."
>
> And when Abraham said: "My Lord, make Thou this a secure land, and provide Thou its people with fruits, whoso among them believes in God and the Last Day," He said: "And whoso denies, him will I let enjoy a little, then will I drive him to the punishment of the Fire; and evil is the journey's end."
>
> And when Abraham and Ishmael raised the foundations of the house: "Our Lord: be Thou accepting of us; Thou art the Hearing, the Knowing.
>
> "Our Lord: make Thou us submitting to Thee, and of our progeny a community submitting to Thee; and show Thou us our rites, and turn Thou towards us; Thou art the Accepting of Repentance, the Merciful.
>
> "Our Lord: raise Thou up among them a messenger from among them who will recite to them Thy proofs, and teach them the Writ and wisdom, and increase them in purity; Thou art the Exalted in Might, the Wise."
>
> And who is averse to the creed of Abraham save he who befools himself? And We chose him in the World; and in the Hereafter he is among the righteous.
>
> When his Lord said to him: "Submit thou," he said: "I have submitted to the Lord of All Creation."

---

63 Arabic: maqam-e-ibrahim.

136

The same did Abraham enjoin upon his sons, as did Jacob:
"O my sons: God has chosen the doctrine for you; so die
not save when you are submitting."
(2:124-132)

(The first house set up for mankind was that at Bakka,
blessed and a guidance for all mankind:
In it are clear proofs of the station of Abraham;[64] and
whoso enters it is safe. And God's claim upon mankind
is a pilgrimage to the house, for whoso is able to find a
path to it; and whoso denies: God is free from need of
all mankind.)
(3:96-97)

The claimed presence of special footprints near a sacred site is not
unique to the religion of Islam. Buddhism makes a similar claim:

The footprint of the Buddha is an imprint of Gautama
Buddha's foot or both feet. There are two forms: natural,
as found in stone or rock, and those made artificially.
Many of the "natural" ones are acknowledged not to be
genuine footprints of the Buddha, but rather replicas
or representations of them, which can be considered
cetiya (Buddhist relics) and also an early aniconic and
symbolic representation of the Buddha.
The footprints of Buddha are on the path from aniconic
to iconic which starts at symbols like the wheel and
moves to statues of Buddha. His footprints are meant to
remind us that Buddha was present on earth and left a
spiritual path to be followed. They are special as they are
the only artifacts that give Buddha a physical presence
on earth as they are actual depressions in the earth. A
depression atop Sri padaya in Sri Lanka is among the
largest and most famous footprints.[65]

---

64 Arabic: maqam-e-ibrahim.
65 "Buddha Footprint." Wikipedia, 27 Feb. 2022, en.wikipedia.org/wiki/Buddha_footprint.

Continuing on with the article of *Hajj* on Wikipedia:

> Tawaf is followed by sa'ay (2:205, 34:5, 53:39), running
> or walking seven times between the hills of Safa and
> Marwah, located near the Kaaba.

Muslims give the general word *sa'ay* a special meaning of *running and walking between two hills*. However, if we check the instances of this word (as given in the article) in the Qur'an we find that this word simply mean *effort* or *endeavor*.

> And when he turns away, he strives[66] in the land working
> corruption therein and destroying tilth and progeny;
> and God loves not corruption.
> (2:205)

> And those who strive[67] against Our proofs, to frustrate:
> those have the punishment of a painful scourge.
> (34:5)

> And that man has not save that for which he strove,[68]
> (53:39)

Another pagan ritual during the *Hajj* which deserves mention is the stoning of the devil. Below is an excerpt on the *Stoning of the Devil* on Wikipedia.

> The Stoning of the Devil (ramy al-jamarāt, lit. "throwing
> of the jamarāt [place of pebbles]")[1][2][3] is part of the
> annual Islamic Hajj pilgrimage to the holy city of Mecca
> in Saudi Arabia. During the ritual, Muslim pilgrims throw
> pebbles at three walls (formerly pillars), called jamarāt,
> in the city of Mina just east of Mecca. It is one of a series
> of ritual acts that must be performed in the Hajj. It is

---

66 Arabic: sa'a.
67 Arabic: sa'aw.
68 Arabic: sa'a.

a symbolic reenactment of Ibrahim's (or Abraham's) hajj, where he stoned three pillars representing the temptation to disobey God.[69]

As expected, this stoning ritual is absent in the Qur'an. However, the idolaters did threaten their messengers with such a punishment.

They said: "O Shuʿayb: we understand not much of what thou sayest; and we consider thee among us as weak. And were it not for thy family, we would have stoned thee; and thou art not to us one respected."
(11:91)

Said he: "Art thou averse to my gods, O Abraham? If thou cease not, I will stone thee; so depart thou from me a good while."
(19:46)

Verses in the Qur'an about hajj

Al-Ṣafā and Al-Marwa are among the tokens of God. So whoso made pilgrimage to the house or visited, he did no wrong to walk around between them; and whoso does good voluntarily, God is grateful and knowing.
(2:158)

They ask thee about the phases of the moon. Say thou: "They are measurements of time for the people and the pilgrimage." And it is not virtue that you approach houses by the backs thereof — but virtue is[...] one who is in prudent fear — but approach houses by the doors thereof; and be in prudent fear of God, that you might be successful.
(2:189)

The inviolable month is for the inviolable month, and the inviolable deeds are just requital: whoso transgressed against you, transgress against him just as he transgressed against you. But be in prudent fear of God, and know that God is with those of prudent fear.

And spend in the cause of God, and give not yourselves over to destruction. And do good; God loves the doers of good.

And complete the pilgrimage and the attendance for God. But if you be straitened, then what is easy of the offering. And shave not your heads until the offering reaches its place of sacrifice. And whoso among you is sick or has a hindrance of the head: the redemption is by fast or charity or penance. And when you are secure, then whoso enjoys the attendance until the pilgrimage, then what is easy of the offering. And whoso has not the means: a fast of three days during the pilgrimage, and seven when you have returned. Those are ten complete. That is for him whose family is not present at the inviolable place of worship. And be in prudent fear of God, and know that God is severe in retribution.

The pilgrimage is in months appointed. And whoso undertakes the pilgrimage therein: no sexual approach, and no perfidy, or quarrelling during the pilgrimage. And whatever good you do, God knows it. And take provision. But the best provision is prudent fear. And be in prudent fear of Me, O you men of understanding.

You do no wrong to seek favour from your Lord. And when you pour forth from ʿArafāt, then remember God at Al-Mashʿar Al-Ḥarām. And remember Him, how He guided you, for indeed you were before it among those astray.

Then pour forth from where men have poured forth. And ask forgiveness of God; God is forgiving and merciful.

And when you have concluded your rites, remember God like your remembrance of your fathers, or with stronger remembrance. And among men is he who says: "Our

Lord: give Thou to us in the World," and he has no portion in the Hereafter.

(2:196-200)

According to 2:196, the *hajj* was in "months appointed". Yet, the
Qur'an does not tell us what or when these months are — it is assumed
the audience at that time knew the timings of this *hajj*. Not to be
deterred, Islam has invented an entire calendar to regulate various
activities including the *hajj*. However, the Qur'an gives us no details of
such a calendar and since we have already established that the Qur'an
is complete, clear, and fully detailed we are, therefore, forced to reject
this Islamic calendar.

> (The first house set up for mankind was that at Bakka,
> blessed and a guidance for all mankind:
> In it are clear proofs of the station of Abraham; and whoso
> enters it is safe. And God's claim upon mankind is a
> pilgrimage to the house, for whoso is able to find a path
> to it; and whoso denies: God is free from need of all
> mankind.)
>
> (3:96-97)

> An acquittal from God and His messenger, to those with
> whom you made a covenant among the idolaters:
> "Travel in the earth four months; and know that you cannot
> escape God, and that God will disgrace the false claimers
> of guidance."
> And a proclamation from God and His messenger to man-
> kind on the day of the greater pilgrimage: "God is free
> of the idolaters, as is His messenger. And if you repent,
> it is better for you; but if you turn away, know that you
> cannot escape God." And bear thou tidings to those who
> ignore warning of a painful punishment,
>
> (9:1-3)

> Have you made the giving of water to the pilgrim and the
> inhabiting of the inviolable place of worship like him

who believes in God and the Last Day and strives in the cause of God? They are not equal before God; and God guides not the wrongdoing people.

(9:19)

Those who ignore warning and turn away from the path of God and the inviolable place of worship which We made for mankind[...]. Alike are the one remaining in it and the one without; and whoso seeks therein deviation by injustice, him will We let taste of a painful punishment.

And when We settled for Abraham the position of the house: "Ascribe thou not a partnership with Me to any-thing; and purify thou My house for those who walk around, and those who stand, and the lowly, and the submitting.

"And proclaim thou among mankind the pilgrimage; they will come to thee on foot, and on every lean mount; they will come from every deep mountain pass,

"That they might witness benefits for them, and remember the name of God on days appointed over their provision of livestock cattle." So eat thereof, and feed the unfor-tunate poor;

Then let them make an end of their unkemptness, and fulfil their vows, and walk around the ancient house.

That[...]. And whoso honours the sacred things of God, it is better for him in the sight of his Lord. And the cattle are lawful to you save that recited to you. And avoid the abomination of idols. And avoid false speech,

Inclining towards God, not ascribing a partnership to Him. And whoso ascribes a partnership to God, it is as if he had fallen from the sky, then the birds snatch him away, or the wind sweeps him away to a far-off place.

That[...]. And whoso honours the tokens of God, then is it from the prudent fear of the hearts.

For you in them are benefits to a stated term; then is their place of sacrifice to the ancient house.

142

And for every community We appointed a rite: that they
remember the name of God over what He has provided
them of livestock cattle. And your God is One God; so
submit to Him. And bear thou glad tidings to the humble:
Whose hearts are afraid when God is remembered, and
those patient over what befalls them, and who uphold
the duty, and of what We have provided them they spend.
And the camels: We appointed them for you among the
tokens of God; for you in them is good. So remember the
name of God over them when they are in lines; and when
their flanks collapse, eat thereof and feed the reticent
poor and the beggar. Thus have We made them subject
for you, that you might be grateful.
(22:25-36)

As you can see there is no mention in the Qur'an of circling a stone
cube idol, running between two hills or stoning the devil. The *hajj*, as
practiced by Abraham, Muhammad and the believers in his time is no
more. It is impossible to re-construct it using the Qur'an. Its format,
time and place were known to the people during the Qur'anic revelation but since this information is not given in the Qur'an, we can safely
conclude that the *hajj* has now passed into antiquity and the duty to
perform it is not applicable to the believers anymore.

12

HADITH LITERATURE

As I have mentioned earlier, the religion of Islam is based primarily on the *hadith* literature. These alleged sayings of the prophet Muhammad, which were written down centuries after his death, are graded by their authenticity.[70] The existence of a grading system is evidence that the earlier Muslims did not entirely trust these *hadiths*. Not surprisingly, the two dominant sects of Islam, Sunni and Shia, have their own sets of *hadith* books.

We have already established that the Qur'an is sufficient guidance for a sincere man wishing to serve God alone. However, the Qur'an does not contain the fundamental pillars and rituals which make up the Islamic religion. In order to attach their invented religion to the Qur'an, the architects of Islam used the *hadith* literature as a back-door. By taking keywords in the Qur'an (*salaat, zakat, hajj* etc.) and giving them specific sectarian definitions via the *hadith* literature, they were able to import their religion into the Qur'an and provide legitimacy for their idolatrous practices.[71] Thus, a general word such as *sujud* — which simply means *submission* — was given a specific meaning of *prostration towards the Kaaba* via the *hadith*. The fact of the matter is that the Qur'an was the only thing revealed to Muhammad and he himself was following it alone.

70 There is no grading system for the Qur'an's verses because God has promised to protect it (15:9). God did not make such a promise for the *hadith* literature.
71 I thank Brother Gerrans for this insight.

Say thou: "I say not to you: 'I possess the treasuries of
God,' or: 'I know the Unseen,' nor do I say to you: 'I am
an angel.' I follow only what is revealed to me." Say thou:
"Are the blind and the seeing equal?" Will you then not
take thought!

And warn thou thereby those who fear that they will be
gathered to their Lord, — they have no ally or intercessor besides Him — that they might be in prudent fear.
(6:50-51)

And when Our proofs are recited to them as clear signs,
those who look not for the meeting with Us say: "Bring
thou a Qur'an other than this; or change thou it." Say
thou: "It is not for me to change it of my own accord.
I follow only what is revealed to me. I fear, if I should
disobey my Lord, the punishment of a tremendous day."
(10:15)

We best know what they say; and thou art not a tyrant
over them. But remind thou with the Qur'an him who
fears My warning.
(50:45)

A revelation from the Lord of All Creation!
(And had he ascribed to Us any sayings,
We would have seized him by the right hand.
Then would We have cut from him the aorta,
And not one of you could have protected him.)
And it is a reminder to those of prudent fear;
(69:43-48)

Making forbidden what God has allowed

Say thou: "Have you seen what God has sent down for
you of provision, and you have made thereof lawful
and unlawful?" Say thou: "Did God give you leave, or is
it about God that you invent?"

And what will those who invent lies about God think on
the Day of Resurrection? God is bountiful to mankind,
but most of them are not grateful.
(10:59-60)

It is a serious matter to allow what God has forbidden and to forbid what
God has allowed. The religion of Islam has a whole list of allowed and
forbidden things which are not mentioned in the Qur'an. For example,
Muslims are forbidden men from wearing silk and gold jewelery but
this prohibition is not mentioned in the Qur'an.

Narrated on the authority of Hudhaifa: The Prophet (peace
be upon him) has prohibited us from drinking and eating
from gold and silver cups and also prohibited us from
the wearing and sitting on fabrics made out of silk.
(*Sahih Bukhari*, Volume 7, Book 72, Number 728)

Say thou: "Who has made unlawful the adornment of God
which He brought forth for His servants, and the good
things of provision?" Say thou: "These are for those who
heed warning in the life of this world exclusively on the
Day of Resurrection." Thus do We set out and detail the
proofs for people who know.
(7:32)

And add not to what your tongues describe the lie: "This
is lawful, and this is unlawful," to invent lies about God;
those who invent lies about God will not succeed:
A brief enjoyment, and they have a painful punishment.
(16:116-117)

There are numerous *hadiths* that contradict each other.[72] The Qur'an,
however, when considered with care, contains no contradictions. That
is because the former is written by men and the latter revealed by God.

72 Anas reported Allah's Apostle (may peace be upon him) disapproved the drinking of
water while standing. (*Sahih Muslim* 23:5017) Ibn Abbas reported: I served. (water of)
Zamzam to Allah's Messenger (may peace be upon him), and he drank it while standing.
(*Sahih Muslim* 23:5023)

(Will they then not consider the Qur'an with care! And
had it been from other than God, they would have found
therein much contradiction.)

(4:82)

Arguments against Qur'an Alone

Obey God and Obey the Messenger

In defense of their *hadith* literature, Muslims point to Qur'anic verses
that command the believers to "obey God and the Messenger." I agree
that believers must obey God and the messenger. But how can we
realistically[73] apply this command today? Obviously, Muhammad is not
among us anymore; he is dead. How can we obey a dead person? We
cannot. Like many other Qur'anic commandments which could only
be applied by believers during Muhammad's time, the command to
"obey God and the Messenger" was for Muhammad's contemporaries.
Consider the following:

O you who heed warning: enter not the houses of the
Prophet, save that leave be given to you for a meal,
without watching for its hour. But when you are called,
then enter; and when you have eaten, then disperse.
And seek not to remain for conversation; that hinders
the Prophet, and he is shy of you; but God is not shy of
the truth. And when you ask of his wives an item: ask it
of them from behind a partition; that is purer for your
hearts and their hearts. And it is not for you to hinder
the messenger of God, or to marry his wives after him
ever; that were, in the sight of God, monstrous.

(33:53)

The believers are but those who believe in God and His
messenger, and when they are with him on a common

73 I say realistically because the Muslims' claim that there are following the messenger
by following suspect literature about his alleged sayings and actions (which he never saw
or approved) is childish.

matter, go not away until they ask leave of him. They who ask leave of thee: those are they who believe in God and His messenger. So when they ask leave of thee for some matter of theirs, give thou leave to whom thou wilt among them, and ask thou forgiveness of God for them; God is forgiving and merciful.

Make not the calling of the Messenger among yourselves as your call one of another. God knows those who slip away surreptitiously among you. And let those who oppose His command beware lest a means of denial befall them, or there befall them a painful punishment.

(24:62-63)

To obey the messenger, after his death, is to follow the one thing that was revealed to him by God i.e. the Qur'an. It is to continue in his tradition of delivering God's message to mankind.

Say thou: "Obey God and obey the Messenger." Then if you turn away, then upon him is what he has been given to bear, and upon you is what you have been given to bear. And if you obey him, you will be guided. And upon the Messenger is only the clear notification,

(God has promised those who heed warning among you and do righteous deeds that He will make them successors in the earth, even as He made those successors who were before them. And He will establish for them their doctrine which He approved for them, and will give them in exchange after their fear, safety. They serve Me; they ascribe not a partnership with Me to anything — and whoso denies after that: — it is they who are the perfidious.)

And uphold the duty and render the purity, and obey the Messenger, that you might obtain mercy.

(24:54-56)

And strive for God with the striving due Him. He has chosen you, and has not placed upon you in doctrine

any distress — the creed of your father Abraham. He
named you those submitting before, and in this, that the
Messenger might be a witness to you, and that you might
be witnesses to men. So uphold the duty, and render the
purity, and hold fast to God; He is your protector. Then
excellent is the Protector! And excellent is the Helper!
(22:78)

Take what the Messenger gives you

Muslims claim that Muhammad was a law-giver — he allowed and
forbade things — but the fact of the matter is that God, alone, is the
law-giver. Muhammad's job was to deliver and follow the Qur'an alone.
The doctors of the law deceptively use the following verse to bolster
their claim, but you can see clearly that this verse is not talking about
Muhammad in the context of a law-giver, it concerns the spoils of war.

What God gave in spoil to His messenger from the people
of the cities belongs to God and His messenger, and to
relatives, and the fatherless, and the needy, and the wayfarer[...] that it be not a distribution by turns between
the rich among you. And what the Messenger gives you:
take it, and from what he forbids you: refrain — and be
in prudent fear of God; God is severe in retribution —
(59:7)

Muhammad Explained the Qur'an

Muslims claim that they need the *hadith* literature because it explains
the Qur'an thereby implying that it was Muhammad's job to explain it.
However, the Qur'an claims that it, itself, is an explanation.

And the day We raise in every community a witness against
them from themselves, and We bring thee as a witness
against these[...]. And We sent down the Writ upon thee
as a clarification of all things, and as guidance, and as a
mercy, and as glad tidings for those submitting. (16:89)

Muhammad's task was not to explain the Qur'an but, like the messengers before him, to deliver God's messages.

> And if they argue with thee, then say thou: "I have submitted my face to God, as have those who follow me." And say thou to those given the Writ and to the unschooled: "Have you submitted?" And if they have submitted, then are they guided; but if they turn away, then upon thee is only the notification; and God sees the servants.
> (3:20)

> And obey God and obey the Messenger, and beware; but if you turn away, then know that upon Our messenger is only the clear notification.
> (5:92)

> Upon the Messenger is only the notification; and God knows what you reveal and what you conceal.
> (5:99)

> And whether We show thee part of what We promise them, or We take thee, but upon thee is the notification; and upon Us is the reckoning.
> (13:40)

> And those who ascribe a partnership say: "Had God willed, we would not have served, besides Him, anything — neither we nor our fathers — nor would we have forbidden anything contrary to Him"; thus did those before them. Then is there upon the messengers save the clear notification?
> (16:35)

> And if they turn away, upon thee is only the clear notification.
> (16:82)

In this[74] is a notification for people who serve.

(21:106)

And We sent thee only as a bearer of glad tidings and a
warner.

(25:56)

So be thou patient, as those of determination among the
messengers were patient, and seek thou not to hasten
for them. The day they see what they are promised,
it will be as though they had not tarried an hour of a
day. Notification! And will there be destroyed save the
perfidious people?

(46:35)

And obey God, and obey the Messenger; but if you turn
away — then upon Our messenger is only the clear
notification.

(64:12)

Say thou: "None will grant me protection against God, nor
will I find, besides Him, a refuge
"Save notification from God and His messages." And whoso
opposes God and His messenger, for him is the fire of
Gehenna; they abiding eternally therein forever.

(72:22-23)

The Qur'an is Difficult to Understand

Muslims claim that the Qur'an is in Arabic and thus can only truly be
understood by a native Arabic speaker. If this was the case, all native
Arab speakers would be guided. The truth of it is that Qur'an is a message to all of mankind[75] and it is not the mastery of the Arabic language
but God's will whether a man is guided or not.

---

74 The Qur'an.
75 See 4:1.

It is a noble recitation
In a hidden Writ,
— None will touch it save those purified—
(56:77-79)

The majority of men are unable to grasp the message of the Qur'an because they are under God's punishment; God has made His Scripture incomprehensible to them. But for those upon whom God has had mercy, the Qur'an is an open book.

Said He: "O Moses: I have chosen thee above mankind, by My messages and by My words; so hold thou to what I have given thee, and be thou among the grateful."

And We wrote for him on the tablets every thing as an admonition and an explanation for everything: "Hold thou them fast, and command thou thy people to take the best thereof. I will show thee the abode of the perfidious:

"I will divert from My proofs those who wax proud in the earth without cause; and if they see every proof believe in it not; and if they see the path of sound judgment take it not as a path, but if they see the path of error take it as a path. For it is that they denied Our proofs and were heedless of them!"

And those who deny Our proofs and the meeting of the Hereafter: their works are vain; will they be rewarded save for what they did?
(7:144-147)

Those who deny the remembrance when it has come to them[...]. And it is a mighty Writ
— Falsehood cannot reach it from before it or from after it — a revelation from One wise and praiseworthy.

Nothing is said to thee but what has been said to the messengers before thee: — "Thy Lord is possessor of forgiveness, and possessor of painful retribution," —

And had We made it a recitation in a foreign tongue, they would have said: "Oh, that its proofs were but set out

and detailed — a foreign tongue and an Arab!" Say thou:
"It is for those who heed warning a guidance and a
healing"; but those who do not believe: in their ears is
deafness, and it is for them blindness; those: they are
called from a far place.

(41:41-44)

Muhammad was given special Wisdom

Muslims claim that God gave Muhammad special "Wisdom" besides the
Qur'an. This argument, like most of the Muslims' arguments, assumes
that the Qur'an is not clear, complete, and fully detailed. Muslims point
to the following verses in support of their claim:

Like as I have sent to you a messenger from among you
reciting to you Our proofs and increasing you in purity
and teaching you the Writ and wisdom and teaching
you what you knew not,

(2:151)

God indeed showed favour to the believers when He
raised up among them a messenger among themselves, reciting to them His proofs, and increasing
them in purity, and teaching them the Writ and wisdom — though they were before in manifest error.

(3:164)

He it is that raised up among the unschooled a messenger from among them, reciting to them His proofs, and
increasing them in purity, and teaching them the Writ
and wisdom — though they were before in manifest
error —

(62:2)

A superficial reading seems to support the Muslims' claim that
Muhammad received "wisdom" besides the Qur'an, but let us investigate

further by looking at some other verses in which the word *wisdom*[76] is used.

> And remember what is recited within your houses of the proofs of God and of wisdom; God is subtle and aware.
> (33:34)

> And there has come to them of reports that wherein is deterrence:
> Far-reaching wisdom; but the warnings avail not.
> (54:4-5)

> And when you divorce women, and they have reached their term, then retain them according to what is fitting or release them according to what is fitting. And retain them not through harm, to transgress; and whoso does that has wronged himself. And take not the proofs of God in mockery; and remember the favour of God upon you, and what He has sent down to you of the Writ and wisdom whereby He admonishes you. And be in prudent fear of God, and know that God knows all things.
> (2:231)

We see the same tactic of assigning special values to general terms in the Qur'an at play again. The Qur'an uses the word *wisdom* in a general sense only and to assign it a meaning of *divine knowledge given to Muhammad besides the Qur'an* is to twist its meaning.

We must go to Muhammad for Judgment

Another argument put forth by Muslims is that God commands the believers to go to the Messenger for judgment. Let us look at the verses in question.

---

76 Arabic: hikmah.

And they say: "We believe in God and the Messenger, and
  we obey"; then a faction among them turns away after
  that — and those are not believers.

And when they are invited to God and His messenger,
  that he judge between them, then a faction among them
  turns away.

But if the truth be theirs, they come to him in willing
  submission.

Is there in their hearts a disease? If they doubt, or fear
  that God would deal unjustly with them — or would His
  messenger: — nay, it is they who are the wrongdoers.

The only word of the believers, when they are invited to
  God and His messenger, that he judge between them, is
  that they say: "We hear and we obey," — and it is they
  who are the successful.

And whoso obeys God and His messenger, and fears God,
  and is in prudent fear of Him: — it is they who are the
  attainers of success.

(24:47-52)

It is clear from the surrounding context that this refers to a faction
who did not come to the Messenger for judgment *during his lifetime.*
Since the Messenger is dead, these verse are inapplicable to the believers. Besides, the scripture with which he was to judge by was the Qur'an
itself. Notice how the Jews were chided for not judging by the Torah (the
Scripture of God which was with them) in their time. Muslims should
heed God's commands and judge by the Qur'an and only the Qur'an.

And how come they to thee for judgment when they have
  the Torah wherein is the judgment of God, then turn
  away after that? And those are not believers.

We sent down the Torah wherein is guidance and light. The
  prophets who submitted judged thereby those who hold
  to Judaism as did the rabbis and the religious scholars
  with what they were given charge of the Writ of God
  and were thereto witnesses: "So fear not mankind but
  fear Me; and sell not My proofs at a cheap price." And

whoso judges not by what God has sent down, it is they who are the false claimers of guidance.

And We prescribed for them therein a life for a life, and an eye for an eye, and a nose for a nose, and an ear for an ear, and a tooth for a tooth, and for wounds just requital; but whoso forgives it by way of charity, it is an expiation for him. And whoso judges not by what God has sent down: it is they who are the wrongdoers.

And We sent Jesus, son of Mary in their footsteps confirming what was before him of the Torah; and We gave him the Gospel wherein was guidance and light, both confirming what was before him of the Torah and as guidance and admonition for those of prudent fear.

And let the people of the Gospel judge by what God sent down therein; and whoso judges not by what God has sent down: it is they who are the perfidious.

And We sent down to thee the Writ with the truth, confirming what is before it of the Writ, and as a control over it. So judge thou between them by what God has sent down; and follow thou not their vain desires away from what has come to thee of the truth. For each of you We appointed an ordinance and a procedure. And had God willed, He could have made you one community; but that He might try you in what He gave you[...]. — So vie in good deeds; unto God will you return all together, and He will inform you of that wherein you differed —

And judge thou between them by what God has sent down; and follow thou not their vain desires, and beware thou of them lest they seduce thee away from some of what God has sent down to thee. And if they turn away, know thou that God but intends to afflict them for some of their transgressions; and many among men are perfidious.

Is it the judgment of ignorance they seek? And who is better than God in judgment for people who are certain?

(5:43-50)

Accept some hadith and reject others

Some Muslims, after realizing that some *hadiths* contradict the Qur'an or contradict each other, propose a compromise: accept those *hadiths* that agree with the Qur'an and reason. However, if they claim that the *hadith*[77] is part of their doctrine, and they are sincere, then they must accept every single *hadith*; there can be no half-measures. The sane approach is to take all of the Qur'an — and only the Qur'an — as the basis for guidance and law:

> Then are you those who kill your own, and turn a faction among you out of their homes, assisting one another against them in sin and enmity; and if they come to you as captives, you ransom them, but unlawful for you was their expulsion. Do you believe in part of the Writ and deny part? Then what is the reward of him among you who does that save disgrace in the life of this world? And on the Day of Resurrection they are sent back to the harshest punishment; and God is not unmindful of what you do.
>
> (2:85)

> He it is that sent down upon thee the Writ; among it are explicit proofs: they are the foundation of the Writ; and others are ambiguous. Then as for those in whose hearts is deviation: they follow what is ambiguous thereof, seeking the means of denial, and seeking its interpretation. And no one knows its interpretation save God, and those firm in knowledge; they say: "We believe in it; all is from our Lord." But only those of insight take heed.
>
> (3:7)

The Qur'an was compiled after Muhammad's death

Muslims claim that Qur'an was compiled in the form of a book after Muhammad's death and, to bolster this claim, they make an even

---

77 The six canonical books of Hadith collection in the case of Sunnis.

stranger claim: Muhammad was illiterate; that he was an *ummiyi* (illiterate) and present the following verse in support of this claim:

> Say: "O men! I am sent unto you all, as the Messenger of Allah, to Whom belongeth the dominion of the heavens and the earth: there is no god but He: it is He That giveth both life and death. So believe in Allah and His Messenger, the Unlettered Prophet, who believeth in Allah and His words: follow him that (so) ye may be guided."
> (7:158)

The above translation by Yusuf Ali (a traditional translator) translates the Arabic word *al-ummiyi* as *Unlettered*. However, a pan-textual analysis of this term means those who are ignorant of the *Writ* i.e. those unlearned about God's Law. Muhammad was an Arab, a people who — unlike the Jews — were *ummiyi* because no Scripture had been revealed to them previously.

> He it is that raised up among the *unschooled* a messenger from among them, reciting to them His proofs, and increasing them in purity, and teaching them the Writ and wisdom — though they were before in manifest error —
> (62:2)

> And among them are those *unschooled*: they know not the Writ save vain desires; and they are only assuming.
> (2:78)

> And if they argue with thee, then say thou: "I have submitted my face to God, as have those who follow me." And say thou to those given the Writ and to the *unschooled*: "Have you submitted?" And if they have submitted, then are they guided; but if they turn away, then upon thee is only the notification; and God sees the servants.
> (3:20)

The Qur'an itself testifies to the fact that it was being codified in the form of a book as it was being revealed to Muhammad.

> By a Writ inscribed
> In a parchment unrolled!
> (52:2-3)

> No, indeed! It is a reminder,
> So whoso wills might remember it,
> In honoured pages,
> Exalted and purified,
> By the hands of scribes
> Noble and virtuous.
> (80:11-16)

The inventors of the religion of Islam first legitimized the false idea that the Qur'an was compiled by Muhammad's companions after his death. Then they argued that the same companions were responsible for transmitting Muhammad's sayings and actions — which were then later on codified in the *hadith* literature. Using this trick, they were able to effectively neutralize those who opposed the *hadith* literature. The fact of the matter is that the Qur'an was compiled during Muhammad's lifetime whereas the *hadith* was compiled centuries after his death. Muhammad did not leave it to others to compile the Qur'an.

Usage of the word hadith in the Qur'an

The Qur'an's usage of the word *hadith* is itself at odds with its meaning claimed by the religion of Islam. The Qur'an uses the word *hadith*[78] to mean *narration, story* or *account.* It never uses it to mean *a saying of the prophet Muhammad.*

> Have they not considered the dominion of the heavens
>   and the earth, and what things God has created, and

---

[78] A full list of verses containing the word *hadith*: 4:42, 4:78, 4:87, 4:140, 6:68, 7:185, 12:6, 12:21, 12:101, 12:111, 18:6, 20:9, 23:44, 31:6, 33:53, 34:19, 39:23, 45:6, 51:24, 52:34, 53:59, 56:81, 66:3, 68:44, 77:50, 79:15, 85:17, 88:1.

that it may be that their term has drawn nigh? And in
what *narration* after this will they believe?
(7:185)

There is in their story a lesson for men of understanding;
it is not an invented *narrative* but a confirmation of
what is before it, and an exposition of every thing, and
guidance, and a mercy for people who believe.
(12:111)

And among men is he who purchases the diversion of
narration to lead astray from the path of God without
knowledge, and takes it in mockery: those have a humiliating punishment.
(31:6)

God has sent down the best *narration*: a Writ of paired
comparison whereat shiver the skins of those who fear
their Lord; then their skins and their hearts soften to
the remembrance of God — that is the guidance of God
wherewith He guides whom He wills;and whom God
sends astray, for him there is no guide.
(39:23)

Those are the proofs of God; We recite them to thee in
truth. Then in what *narration* after God and His proofs
will they believe?
(45:6)

Is it then this *narration* you disdain
And make denial thereof your livelihood?
(56:81-82)

Then in what *narration* after it will they believe?
(77:50)

Usage of the word sunnah in the Qur'an

Similarly, the Qur'an uses the word *sunnah*[79] to mean *practice* or *precedent*; it never uses it to mean *the practice of Muhammad*.

> Say thou to those who ignore warning: if they cease, what is past will be forgiven them; but if they return, then the *practice* of the former peoples has gone before.
> (8:38)

> They believe not in it; and the *practice* of the former peoples has passed away.
> (15:13)

> The practice of those We sent before thee of Our messengers[...]; and thou wilt not find in Our *practice* any alteration.
> (17:77)

> And there prevented men from believing when the guidance came to them, and from asking forgiveness of their Lord, only that the *practice* of the former peoples should come to them, or the punishment should come to them face to face.
> (18:55)

> There is no blame upon the Prophet concerning what God ordained for him. The *practice* of God among those who passed away before — and the command of God is a destiny decreed —
> (33:38)
> The *practice* of God among those who passed away before[...]; and thou wilt not find for the *practice* of God any replacement.
> (33:62)

---

79 A full list of verses containing the word *sunnah* can be found here: 3:137, 4:26, 8:38, 15:13, 17:77, 18:55, 33:38, 33:62, 35:43, 40:85, 48:23.

Waxing proud in the land, and scheming evil; but the evil
scheme surrounds none save its authors. Then look
they save for the *practice* of the former peoples? And
thou wilt not find in the *practice* of God any change; and
thou wilt not find in the *practice* of God any alteration.
(35:43)

The truth of the matter is that the Muslims —like the Jews before
them — have abandoned God's scripture.

And there followed after them successors who inherited
the Writ, taking the goods of this fleeting life, and saying:
"It will be forgiven us." And if there come to them goods
the like thereof, they will take them. Has there not been
taken from them an agreement to the Writ, that they
ascribe not to God save the truth, and that they study
what is therein? And the abode of the Hereafter is better
for those of prudent fear. Will you then not use reason!
And those who hold fast the Writ, and uphold the duty —
We cause not to be lost the reward of those who do right.
(7:169-170)

13

THE SALAAT

Muslims claim that God commanded the prophet Muhammad to uphold a ritual prayer — called the *salaat* — five times a day. However, the Qur'an does not contain step-by-step instructions on how to perform this important ritual. That is because the Qur'an uses the word *salaat* in a generic sense to mean *duty*.[80] While remembering God is the primary duty of every believer, there are other duties which are incumbent upon him as well.

> *alif lām mīm*
> That is the Writ about which there is no doubt, a guidance
>   to those of prudent fear:
> Those who believe in the Unseen, and uphold the *salaat*,
>   and of what We have provided them they spend;
> And those who believe in what was sent down to thee, and
>   what was sent down before thee, and of the Hereafter
>   they are certain:
> Those are upon guidance from their Lord; and it is they
>   who are the successful.
>
> (2:1-5)

We see the usage of *salaat* in the episode of Moses' first encounter with God where it is clear that God was commanding Moses to establish the *duty* to remember Him; the primary duty of every believer.

---

80 I am indebted to Sam Gerrans for this insight.

"I am God. There is no god save I, so serve thou Me; and
uphold thou the *salaat* for My remembrance:
"The Hour is coming — I almost conceal it — that every
soul might be rewarded for that for which it strives;
"And let not turn thee away from it him who believes not
in it but follows his vain desire, or thou wilt perish.
(20:14-16)

The Qur'an details Moses' first encounter with God in two other places[81] and nowhere are the details of a specific ritual prayer present. Moses was simply being commanded to uphold the duty to remember God.

In the following exchange between the unbelievers and the messenger Shuʿayb, the unbelievers are asking Shuʿayb whether his *duty* commands him to leave what his ancestors served. Shuʿayb's duty as a messenger and a believer was to study and warn with the Scripture he was sent with. It was in this context of warning the unbelievers that they argued with Shuʿayb whether the Scripture he was sent with commanded him to forsake the practices of his forefathers.

And to Madyan, their brother Shuʿayb: he said: "O my people: serve God; you have no god but He; so decrease not the measure and the balance. I see you in affluence, but I fear for you the punishment of an encompassing day."
And: "O my people: fulfil the measure and the balance with equity, and deprive not men of their possessions, and commit not evil in the earth, working corruption.
"The remainder of God is better for you, if you be believers. And I am not a custodian over you."
They said: "O Shuʿayb: does thy *salaat* command thee that we leave what our fathers served, or that we do not with our wealth what we will? Thou art the clement, the right-minded!"
(11:84-87)

---

81 See 27:9, 28:30.

164

It is evidently clear that in this context that the messenger Shuʿayb was reading the Scripture and warning his people and not performing a ritual prayer.

What does yusalli mean?

Perhaps the biggest problem with the idea of *salaat* as a ritual prayer is that the Qur'an says God performs the *salaat* for the believers. At this juncture, traditional translators abandon the value of *salaat* as a *ritual prayer* altogether; it does not befit God to perform a ritual prayer — Glory be unto Him! Both of the following verses feature the same Arabic word *yusalli,* but Yusuf Ali (a traditional translator) translates it differently due to his understanding of *salaat* as a *ritual prayer.*

> He it is Who sends blessings[82] on you, as do His angels, that He may bring you out from the depths of Darkness into Light: and He is Full of Mercy to the Believers.
> (33:43)

> While he[83] was standing in prayer[84] in the chamber, the angels called unto him: "Allah doth give thee glad tidings of Yahya, witnessing the truth of a Word from Allah, and (be besides) noble, chaste, and a prophet, — of the (goodly) company of the righteous."
> (3:39)

In the above two verses, the same word *yusalli*[85] is used; which literally means *he does salaat.* Yusuf Ali translates it as *blessings* when it refers to God[86] and *prayer* when it refers to a man.[87] However, when we translate salaat as duty this problem is resolved. In 33:43, God is doing *His duty* for the believers by bringing them "out of darkness into the light." In 3:39, the prophet Zachariah was doing his duty of

---

82 Arabic: yusalli.
83 Prophet Zachariah.
84 Arabic: yusalli.
85 Root: s-l-w.
86 See 33:43.
87 See 3:39.

supplicating to God.

> O you who heed warning: remember God with much
> remembrance,
> And give glory to Him morning and evening.
> He it is that performs the *duty* for you, as do His angels,
> that He might bring you out of darkness into the light;
> and He is merciful to the believers.
> Their greeting the day they meet Him will be: "Peace!"
> And He has prepared for them a noble reward.
>   (33:41-44)

> So her Lord accepted her with a comely acceptance, and
> caused her to grow with a comely growth, and placed her
> in the charge of Zachariah. Whenever Zachariah entered
> upon her in the chamber, he found with her provision.
> He said: "O Mary: whence comes this to thee?" She said:
> "It is from God; God gives provision to whom He wills
> without reckoning."
> Thereupon Zachariah called to his Lord, saying: "My Lord:
> give Thou me from Thyself goodly progeny; Thou art
> the hearer of supplication."
> And the angels called to him as he stood performing the
> *duty* in the chamber: "God gives thee glad tidings of
> John, confirming a word from God, both honourable and
> chaste, and a prophet among the righteous."
>   (3:37-39)

Types of salaat

Having established that *salaat* means *duty*, we shall now look at the various duties that a believer is commanded to uphold. Besides the primary duty of remembering God, a believer must adhere to other duties such as reading the Qur'an, supplicating to God alone and warning others.

Remember God

alif lām mīm

That is the Writ about which there is no doubt, a guidance
to those of prudent fear:

Those who believe in the Unseen, and uphold the duty,
and of what We have provided them they spend;

And those who believe in what was sent down to thee, and
what was sent down before thee, and of the Hereafter
they are certain:

Those are upon guidance from their Lord; and it is they
who are the successful.

(2:1-5)

O children of Israel: remember My favour wherewith I
favoured you; and fulfil the covenant with Me, and I
will fulfil the covenant with you; and Me — be you in
fear of Me.

And believe in what I have sent down confirming what is
with you, and be not the first to deny it; and sell not My
proofs at a cheap price; and Me — be you in prudent
fear of Me.

And clothe not truth with vanity, nor conceal the truth
when you know.

And uphold the duty, and render the purity, and be lowly
with the lowly.

Enjoin you virtue upon mankind, and forget yourselves
when you recite the Writ? Will you then not use reason!

And seek help in patience and duty; and it is hard save
for the humble:

Those who consider that they will meet their Lord, and
that to Him they are returning.

(2:40-46)

And when We took an agreement of the children of Israel:
"Serve not save God; and towards parents good conduct,
and towards kin, and the fatherless, and the poor; and

speak kindly to men; and uphold the duty, and render the purity," then you turned away save a few among you; and you are averse.

And when We took your agreement: "Shed not your blood, and turn not your own out of your homes," then you affirmed and bore witness;

Then are you those who kill your own, and turn a faction among you out of their homes, assisting one another against them in sin and enmity; and if they come to you as captives, you ransom them, but unlawful for you was their expulsion. Do you believe in part of the Writ and deny part? Then what is the reward of him among you who does that save disgrace in the life of this world? And on the Day of Resurrection they are sent back to the harshest punishment; and God is not unmindful of what you do.

Those are they who bought the life of this world at the price of the Hereafter, so the punishment will not be lightened for them, nor will they be helped.

(2:83-86)

Many among the doctors of the Law wish to turn you back as atheists after your faith out of envy from their souls after the truth has become clear to them. But pardon and forbear until God brings His command; God is over all things powerful.

And uphold the duty, and render the purity; and what good you send ahead for your souls, you will find it with God; God sees what you do.

(2:109-110)

So remember Me, I will remember you; and be grateful to Me, and deny Me not.

O you who heed warning: seek help in patience and duty; God is with the patient.

(2:152-153)

168

It is not virtue that you turn your faces towards the East and the West. But virtue is: one who believes in God, and the Last Day, and the angels, and the Writ, and the prophets, and gives wealth in spite of love of it to relatives, and the fatherless, and the needy, and the wayfarer, and those who ask, and to manumit slaves; and who upholds the duty, and renders the purity; and those who keep their covenant when they make a covenant; and the patient in affliction and adversity, and during conflict: those are they who are sincere; and it is they who are those of prudent fear.
(2:177)

Those who consume usury will not stand save as stands he whom the satan buffets with his touch; for it is that they say: "Commerce is but the same as usury," when God has made commerce lawful and forbidden usury! And he to whom came the admonition from his Lord, and desisted: he has what is past, and his case is with God. But whoso returns: those are the companions of the Fire; therein they abide eternally.
God eliminates usury, and increases charity; and God loves not every ingrate and sinner.
Those who heed warning and do righteous deeds, and uphold the duty, and render the purity: they have their reward with their Lord; and no fear will be upon them, nor will they grieve.
O you who heed warning: be in prudent fear of God; and give up what remains of usury, if you be believers.
(2:275-278)

Preserve the duties[88] — and the median duty — and stand up for God, humbly obedient;
And if you fear, then walking or riding. But when you are secure, then remember God as He taught you what you knew not. (2:238-239)

88 See verses above this verse to see what those duties are.

Hast thou not considered those to whom it was said: "Restrain your hands; and uphold the duty, and render the purity," but when fighting is prescribed for them, then a faction among them fears men like the fear of God, or a stronger fear? And they said: "Our Lord: why hast Thou prescribed fighting for us? Oh, that Thou wouldst but delay us a little while!" Say thou: "Little is the enjoyment of the World"; and the Hereafter is better for him who is in prudent fear; and you will not be wronged a hair upon a date-stone.
(4:77)

And when you are travelling in the earth, you do no wrong to cut short some of the duty if you fear that those who ignore warning will subject you to means of denial — the false claimers of guidance are an open enemy to you —
And when thou art among them, uphold thou the duty for them; then let there stand a number of them with thee, and let them take their arms; then when they have submitted, let them be behind you and let another number come that has not performed the duty, and let them perform the duty with thee; and let them take their precautions and their arms. (Those who ignore warning wish that you would neglect your arms and your equipment, so they might assault you in a single assault; but you do no wrong if there is a hindrance to you from rain or you are sick, that you lay aside your arms; but take your precautions: God has prepared for the false claimers of guidance a humiliating punishment.)
And when you have concluded the duty, remember God standing, and sitting, and upon your sides, and when you are at ease; but uphold the duty — the duty is upon the believers a time-limited Writ —
(4:101-103)

The waverers seek to deceive God, but He is deceiving
them; and when they rise up for the duty, they rise up
to be seen of men, and remember not God save a little,
Wavering in-between — neither to these, nor to those;
and he whom God causes to go astray, thou wilt not
find for him a path.
(4:142-143)

So, for injustice among those who hold to Judaism, We
made unlawful to them good things which had been
lawful to them, and for their turning away from the
path of God much,
And for their taking of usury when they had been forbidden it, and their consuming the wealth of men in vanity;
and We have prepared for the false claimers of guidance
among them a painful punishment.
But those firm in knowledge and the believers among
them believe in what is sent down to thee, and what was
sent down before thee, as do the upholders of the duty,
and the renderers of the purity, and the believers in God
and the Last Day — those will We give a great reward.
(4:160-162)

O you who heed warning: when you rise up for the duty:
wash your faces, and your hands to the elbows, and
wipe your heads, and your feet to the ankles. And if you
are unclean, purify yourselves. And if you were ill, or
on a journey, or one of you came from the privy, or you
have lain with women, then find not water: resort to
clean soil, and wipe your faces and your hands with it.
God wishes not to place any distress upon you; but He
wishes to purify you and to complete His favour upon
you, that you might be grateful.
And remember the favour of God upon you, and His agreement which He agreed with you, when you said: "We
hear and we obey." And be in prudent fear of God; God
knows what is in the breasts. (5:6-7)

O you who heed warning: whoso among you renounces his doctrine: God will bring a people whom He will love, and who will love Him: humble towards the believers; stern towards the false claimers of guidance; striving in the cause of God, and fearing not the reproach of a critic. That is the bounty of God He gives to whom He wills; and God is encompassing and knowing.

Your ally is but God and His messenger, and those who heed warning — those who uphold the duty, and render the purity; and they are lowly —

And whoso takes God and His messenger and those who heed warning as ally: the party of God, they will be the victors.

O you who heed warning: take not those who take your doctrine in mockery and fun among those given the Writ before you and the atheists as allies; and be in prudent fear of God if you be believers.

And when you call to the duty they take it in mockery and fun, for it is that they are people who do not reason!
(5:54-58)

O you who heed warning: wine, and games of chance, and altars, and divining arrows are an abomination of the work of the satan; so avoid it, that you might be successful.

The satan but wishes to cause between you enmity and hatred in wine and the games of chance, and to turn you away from the remembrance of God and from the duty; so will you not desist?

And obey God and obey the Messenger, and beware; but if you turn away, then know that upon Our messenger is only the clear notification.
(5:90-92)

And this is a Writ We have sent down, one blessed, con-firming what was before it, and that thou warn the mother of cities and those around her; and those who

believe in the Hereafter believe in it, and they preserve
their duty.

(6:92)

Say thou: "As for me, my Lord has guided me to a straight
path, a right doctrine, the creed of Abraham, inclining
to truth; and he was not of the idolaters."
Say thou: "My duty and my penance and my living and my
dying are for God, the Lord of All Creation.
"He has no partner, and that have I been commanded; and
I am the first of those submitting."
Say thou: "Is it other than God I should desire as Lord
when He is Lord of all things?" And every soul earns
not save for itself, and no bearer bears the burden of
another; then to your Lord is your return, and He will
inform you of that wherein you differed.
And He it is that made you the successors of the earth,
and raised some of you above others in degree, that He
might try you by what He has given you. Thy Lord is
swift in retribution; and He is forgiving and merciful.

(6:161-165)

They ask thee about the spoils of war. Say thou: "The spoils
of war are for God and the Messenger; so be in prudent
fear of God, and make right in what is between you; and
obey God and His messenger, if you be believers."
The believers are but those who when God is remembered,
their hearts are afraid, and when His proofs are recited
to them, it increases them in faith, and in their Lord they
place their trust,
Those who uphold the duty, and of what We have provided
them they spend:
It is they who are the believers in truth; they have degrees
with their Lord, and forgiveness, and a noble provision

(8:1-4)

But how can they[89] not be punished by God when they
turn away from the inviolable place of worship, and are
not its allies? Its allies are only those of prudent fear;
but most of them know not.

And their duty at the house is only whistling and clapping
— so taste the punishment for what you denied!

(8:34-35)

And when the inviolable months have passed, then kill
the idolaters wheresoever you find them, and seize
them, and restrain them, and lie in wait for them at
every place of ambush. But if they repent, and uphold
the duty, and render the purity, then let them go their
way; God is forgiving and merciful.

And if one of the idolaters seeks thy protection, then grant
thou him protection until he hears the words of God;
then convey thou him to his place of security — is it not
that they are people who know not!

How can there be for the idolaters a covenant with God and
with His messenger save those with whom you made a
covenant at the inviolable place of worship? — so long
as they take a straight path with you, then take a straight
path with them; God loves those of prudent fear —

How, when if they get the better of you, they observe
neither pact of kinship nor obligation to protect? They
please you with their mouths, but their hearts refuse;
and most of them are perfidious.

They have sold the proofs of God at a cheap price and
turned away from His path; evil is what they did.

And they regard towards a believer neither pact of kinship, nor obligation to protect; and it is they who are
the transgressors.

But if they repent, and uphold the duty, and render the
purity, then are they your brethren in doctrine; and
We set out and detail the proofs for people who know.

---

89 Those who ignore warning.

And if they renege on their oaths after their covenant and
revile your doctrine, then fight the leaders of denial:
they have no oaths that they might desist.

Will you not fight a people who broke their oaths, and pur-
posed to turn the Messenger out, and began against you
the first time? Do you fear them? Then God is worthier
that you should fear Him, if you be believers.

Fight them! God will punish them at your hands and disgrace them, and help you against them, and heal the
breasts of people who believe

And remove the wrath of their hearts; and God relents
towards whom He wills; and God is knowing and wise.

If you think that you will be left when God knows not
those among you who have striven, and have taken —
besides God, and His messenger, and the believers — no
confidant[...]. And God is aware of what you do.

It is not for the idolaters to inhabit the places of worship
of God, bearing witness against themselves to denial;
those: their works are vain, and in the Fire do they
abide eternally.

He only inhabits the places of worship of God who believes
in God and the Last Day, and upholds the duty, and renders the purity, and fears not save God; and it may be
that those are of the guided.

(9:5-18)

The wavering men and the wavering women are alike:
they enjoin perversity, and they forbid what is fitting,
and they close their hands; they have forgotten God,
so He has forgotten them. The waverers: they are the
perfidious.

And God has promised the wavering men, and the wavering
women, and the atheists, the fire of Gehenna, they abiding eternally therein; it is sufficient for them. And God
has cursed them; and they have a lasting punishment.

Like those before you, stronger than you in might and
greater in wealth and children: they enjoyed their lot.

And you have enjoyed your lot as they enjoyed their lot who were before you; and you have discoursed vainly like those discoursed vainly; those: their works are vain in the World and the Hereafter; and it is they who are the losers.

Has not the report of those before them come to them: the people of Noah, and ʿĀd, and Thamūd, and the people of Abraham, and the people of Madyan, and the cities thrown down? Their messengers brought them clear signs; and God wronged them not, but they wronged their souls.

And the believing men and the believing women are allies of one another: they enjoin what is fitting, and forbid perversity, and uphold the duty, and render the purity, and obey God and His messenger; those: God will have mercy on them; God is exalted in might and wise.

And God has promised the believing men and the believing women gardens beneath which rivers flow — they abiding eternally therein — and goodly dwellings in gardens of perpetual abode; and approval from God is greater; that is the Great Achievement.

(9:67-72)

And uphold thou the duty at the two ends of the day, and at an approach of the night: good deeds take away evil deeds! — that is a reminder for those who remember —

And be thou patient, for God causes not to be lost the reward of the doers of good.

Oh, that among the generations before you there had but been a remnant forbidding corruption in the land save a few whom We saved among them! But those who did wrong followed what they had been given therein of opulence, and were lawbreakers.

(11:114-116)

Is then he who knows that what is sent down to thee from thy Lord is the truth like him who is blind? There take heed but those of insight:

Those who fulfil the covenant of God, and break not the agreement,

And who join what God commanded to be joined, and fear their Lord, and dread the evil of the reckoning,

And who are patient seeking the face of their Lord, and uphold the duty, and spend of what We have provided them, secretly and openly, and they avert evil with good: those have the good final abode:

(13:19-22)

And they made equals to God, that they might lead astray from His path. Say thou: "Enjoy yourselves, for your journey's end is the Fire."

Say thou to My servants who heed warning, that they uphold the duty, and spend of what We have provided them, secretly and openly, before there comes a day wherein there is neither bargaining nor friendship.

(14:30-31)

And has there come to thee the story of Moses?

When he saw a fire, and said to his people: "Stay here; I perceive a fire. I might bring you therefrom a firebrand, or find at the fire guidance."

And when he came to it, he was called: "O Moses:

"I am thy Lord; so remove thou thy sandals; thou art in the sacred valley of Ṭuwa.

"And I have chosen thee, so hearken thou to what is revealed:

"I am God. There is no god save I, so serve thou Me; and uphold thou the duty for My remembrance:

"The Hour is coming — I almost conceal it — that every soul might be rewarded for that for which it strives;

"And let not turn thee away from it him who believes not
in it but follows his vain desire, or thou wilt perish.
(20:9-16)

And We gave him[90] Isaac, and Jacob in addition; and each
We made righteous,
And We made them leaders, guiding by Our command,
and revealed to them the doing of good deeds, and the
upholding of duty, and the rendering of the purity; and
Us they served.
(21:72-73)

And for every community We appointed a rite: that they
remember the name of God over what He has provided
them of livestock cattle. And your God is One God; so
submit to Him. And bear thou glad tidings to the humble:
Whose hearts are afraid when God is remembered, and
those patient over what befalls them, and who uphold
the duty, and of what We have provided them they spend.
And the camels: We appointed them for you among the
tokens of God; for you in them is good. So remember the
name of God over them when they are in lines; and when
their flanks collapse, eat thereof and feed the reticent
poor and the beggar. Thus have We made them subject
for you, that you might be grateful.
Their flesh does not reach God, nor their blood. But prudent fear reaches Him from you. Thus have We made
them subject for you, that you might magnify God for
guiding you. And bear thou glad tidings to the doers of
good.
God defends those who heed warning; God loves not every
treacherous ingrate.
Leave is given those who are fought because they were
wronged: — and God is able to help them —
Those who have been turned out of their homes without cause save that they said: "Our Lord is God." And

90 Prophet Abraham.

were God not to repel some people by means of others, pious communities would be destroyed, and trade, and duties, and places of worship wherein the name of God is remembered much[...]. But God will help him who helps Him: — God is strong and exalted in might —

Those who, if We establish them in the land, uphold the duty and render the purity, and enjoin what is fitting, and forbid perversity; and to God belongs the final outcome of matters.

(22:34-41)

Those who have been turned out of their homes without cause save that they said: "Our Lord is God." And were God not to repel some people by means of others, pious communities would be destroyed, and trade, and duties, and places of worship wherein the name of God is remembered much[...]. But God will help him who helps Him: — God is strong and exalted in might —

(22:40)

And strive for God with the striving due Him. He has chosen you, and has not placed upon you in doctrine any distress — the creed of your father Abraham. He named you those submitting before, and in this, that the Messenger might be a witness to you, and that you might be witnesses to men. So uphold the duty, and render the purity, and hold fast to God; He is your protector. Then excellent is the Protector! And excellent is the Helper!

(22:78)

And We gave Luqmān wisdom: "Be thou grateful to God." And whoso is grateful, he is but grateful for his soul; and whoso denies — God is free from need and praiseworthy. And when Luqmān said to his son, while he exhorted him: "O my son: ascribe thou not a partnership to God; ascribing partnership is a tremendous injustice."

And We enjoined upon man concerning his parents: — his
mother bore him in weakness upon weakness; and his
weaning is in two years — "Be thou grateful to Me, and
to thy parents; unto Me is the journey's end.
"But if they strive with thee to make thee ascribe a partnership to that of which thou hast no knowledge, then
obey thou them not. And accompany thou them in the
World according to what is fitting; but follow thou the
path of him who turns to Me. Then to Me is your return,
and I will tell you what you did."
"O my son: though it be the weight of a grain of mustard
seed, and it be in a rock, or in the heavens, or in the
earth, God will bring it forth; God is subtle and aware."
"O my son: uphold thou the duty, and enjoin thou what is
fitting, and forbid thou perversity, and be thou patient
over what befalls thee; that is among the resolution of
affairs.
"And turn thou not thy cheek to men, and walk thou not
in the earth haughtily; God loves not every conceited
boaster.
"And be thou modest in thy walk, and lower thou thy voice;
the most loathsome of voices is the voice of the donkey."
(31:12-19)

Successful are the believers:
Those who in their duty are humble,
And those who from vain speech turn away,
And those who act upon the purity.
(23:1-4)

In houses God has given leave to be raised, and His name
to be remembered therein, there give Him glory therein
in the mornings and the evenings
Men whom neither trade nor commerce divert from the
remembrance of God and upholding the duty and rendering the purity. They fear a day wherein the hearts
and the eyes will turn about,

That God might reward them for the best of what they
did, and increase them out of His bounty; and God gives
provision to whom He wills without reckoning.
(24:36-38)

And uphold the duty and render the purity, and obey the
Messenger, that you might obtain mercy.
Think not that those who ignore warning can escape in
the earth; and their shelter is the Fire, and evil is the
journey's end.
O you who heed warning: let ask leave of you those
whom your right hands possess and those who have
not reached puberty among you at three times: before
the duty of the dawn, and when you lay aside your garments at noon, and after the duty of the night: three
times of nakedness for you; you and they do no wrong
beyond them, some of you moving about among others
of you. Thus God makes plain to you the proofs; and God
is knowing and wise.
(24:56-58)

ṭā sīn Those are the proofs of the Qur'an, and of a Clear Writ
As guidance and glad tidings for the believers,
Those who uphold the duty, and render the purity, and of
the Hereafter they are certain.
Those who believe not in the Hereafter, We have made
their deeds fair to them, so they wander blindly.
(27:1-4)

alif lām mīm
Those are the proofs of the Wise Writ
As guidance and mercy for the doers of good:
Those who uphold the duty, and render the purity, and of
the Hereafter are certain:
Those are upon guidance from their Lord; and it is they
who are the successful.
(31:2-5)

O wives of the Prophet: whoso among you commits manifest sexual immorality, for her the punishment is dou-
bled; and that is easy for God.

And whoso among you is humbly obedient to God and
His messenger, and works righteousness, We will give
her her reward twice over; and We have prepared for
her a noble provision.

O wives of the Prophet: you are not like any among women.
If you are in prudent fear, then be not soft in speech lest
he in whose heart is disease should desire; but speak
a fitting word,

And stay within your houses; and display not yourselves
with the display of the former time of ignorance; and
uphold the duty and render the purity, and obey God
and His messenger. God but intends to remove abomination from you — people of the house — and to purify
you completely.

And remember what is recited within your houses of the
proofs of God and of wisdom; God is subtle and aware.
(33:30-34)

Say thou: "I am only a mortal like you. It is revealed to me
that your God is One God. So take a straight path to Him,
and ask forgiveness of Him!" And woe to the idolaters:

Those who render not the purity, and of the Hereafter
they are deniers!

Those who heed warning and do righteous deeds: they
have a reward unending.
(41:6-8)

O you who heed warning: when it is said to you: "Make
room in the assemblies," then make room; God will make
room for you. And when it is said: "Arise," then arise.
God will raise those who heed warning and those given
knowledge among you in degree. And God is aware of
what you do.

O you who heed warning: when you converse confiden-
tially with the Messenger, send ahead charity before
your private conversation. That is better for you, and
purer. But if you find not the means — God is forgiving
and merciful.

Fear you to send ahead charity before your private conversation? Then when you do not — and God has turned
towards you — then uphold the duty and render the
purity, and obey God and His messenger. And God is
aware of what you do.

(58:11-13)

O you who heed warning: when the call is heard for the
duty of the day of assembly, then hasten to the remembrance of God, and leave commerce; that is better for
you, if you but knew.

And when the duty is concluded, disperse in the land, and
seek of the bounty of God; and remember God much
that you might be successful.

(62:9-10)

No, indeed! It is a blazing fire,
Removing the scalp,
Calling him who turned and went away
And gathered and hoarded.
Man was created anxious
— When evil touches him, impatient,
And when good touches him, withholding —
Save the performers of duty:
Those who are constant in their duty,
And those in whose wealth is a due known
For the petitioner and the one deprived,

(70:15-25)

And are those who confirm the Day of Judgment,
And are those who, of the punishment of their Lord, are
in dread,

(The punishment of their Lord is not that from which
   there is safety)
And are those who preserve their chastity
Save with their wives, or what their right hands possess
   — for then are they not blameworthy,
(But whoso seeks beyond that: it is they who are the
   transgressors)
And are those who are to their trusts and their covenant
   attentive,
And are those who, in their witness, are upright,
And are those who preserve their duty:
Those are in gardens, honoured.
                        (70:26-35)

In gardens, they will ask each other
About the lawbreakers:
"What brought you into Saqar?"[91]
They will say: "We were not among the performers of duty,
"And we fed not the needy.
"And we discoursed vainly with those who discourse vainly,
"And denied the Day of Judgment
"Until the Certainty came to us."
                        (74:40-47)

To thy Lord, that day, will be the driving.
For he neither gave credence, nor performed the duty,
But denied and turned away
Then went to his household in arrogance.
                        (75:30-33)

So remind thou; if the reminder should benefit
He will take heed who fears.
But the most wretched will avoid it,
Who will burn in the Great Fire,
Then will he neither die therein nor live.

---

91 Another name for Hell.

He is successful who has purified himself,
And remembers the name of his Lord and performs the
duty.

(87:14-15)

Hast thou seen him who forbids
A servant when he performs the duty?
Hast thou considered if he is upon guidance,
Or enjoins prudent fear?
Hast thou considered if he denies and turns away?
Knows he not that God sees?
No, indeed! If he cease not, We will drag him by the
forelock,
The lying, offending forelock.
Then let him call his council.
We will call the guards of Hell.
No, indeed! Obey thou not him, but submit thou, and
draw thou near.

(96:9-19)

Those who ignore warning among the doctors of the
Law and the idolaters were not to desist until the clear
evidence came to them:
A messenger from God, reciting purified pages
In which are upright writs.
And those given the Writ were divided only after the clear
evidence had come to them.
And they were commanded only to serve God, sincere to
Him in doctrine, inclining to truth; and to uphold the
duty, and to render the purity — and that is the doctrine
of the upright.
Those who ignore warning among the doctors of the
Law and the idolaters will be in the fire of Gehenna,
they abiding eternally therein — it is they who are the
worst of creatures.
Those who heed warning and do righteous deeds — it is
they who are the best of creatures,

Their reward is with their Lord: gardens of perpetual
abode beneath which rivers flow, they abiding eternally
therein forever; God is pleased with them, and they
pleased with Him; that is for him who fears his Lord.
(98:1-8)

We have given thee abundance,
So perform thou the duty to thy Lord, and attain thou
mastery.
He that hates thee — he is the one cut off.
(108:1-3)

Glorify God

So be thou patient over what they say, and give thou glory
with the praise of thy Lord before the rising of the sun,
and before its setting. And some periods of the night
give thou glory; and at the ends of the day, that thou
mightest be satisfied.
And extend thou not thine eyes towards what We have
granted some among them to enjoy — the flower of
the life of this world — that We might subject them to
means of denial therein; and the provision of thy Lord
is better and more enduring.
And enjoin thou upon thy people the duty, and be thou
steadfast therein. We ask thee not for provision; We
provide for thee. And the final outcome is for those of
prudent fear.
(20:130-132)

Dost thou not see that God, to Him gives glory whoso is
in the heavens and the earth, and the birds with wings
outstretched? Each, he knows his duty and his glorification; and God knows what they do.
(24:41)

Call men to God

And when his Lord tried Abraham with words and he fulfilled them, He said: "I will make thee a leader for mankind." Said he: "And of my progeny?" He said: "My covenant does not reach the wrongdoers."

And when We made the house a meeting place for mankind, and a place of security — and make from the station of Abraham a place of duty — and We made a covenant with Abraham and Ishmael: "Purify My house for those who walk around, and those who remain, and the lowly and the submitting."

(2:124-125)

(And when Abraham said: "My Lord: make Thou this land secure; and preserve Thou me and my sons from serving idols.

"My Lord: they have led astray many among mankind. But whoso follows me, he is of me; and whoso disobeys me: Thou art forgiving and merciful.

"Our Lord: I have settled some of my progeny in an uncultivated valley by Thy inviolable house, our Lord, that they uphold the duty; so make Thou hearts among men incline towards them, and provide Thou them some fruits, that they might be grateful.

"Our Lord: Thou knowest what we hide, and what we make known; and nothing is hidden from God in the earth or in the heaven.

"Praise belongs to God who has given me in old age Ishmael and Isaac! My Lord is the hearer of supplication.

"My Lord: make Thou me one upholding the duty, and of my progeny, our Lord, and accept Thou my supplication.

"Our Lord: forgive Thou me, and my parents, and the believers, the day the reckoning takes place.")

(14:35-41)

God's duty to the believers

Who, when calamity befalls them, say: "We belong to God, and to Him are we returning."
Upon those are duties and mercy from their Lord, and it is they who are the guided.
(2:156-157)

O you who heed warning: remember God with much remembrance,
And give glory to Him morning and evening.
He it is that performs the duty for you, as do His angels, that He might bring you out of darkness into the light; and He is merciful to the believers.
(33:43)

Petition God alone

He makes the night enter into the day, and makes the day enter into the night, and He made subject the sun and the moon, each running for a stated term. That is God, your Lord: to Him belongs the dominion; and those to whom you call, besides Him, possess not the skin of a date-stone.
If you call to them, they will not hear your call; and were they to hear, they would not respond to you. And on the Day of Resurrection they will deny your ascription of partnership. And none can inform thee like One Aware.
O mankind: you are in need of God; and God, He is the Free from Need, the Praiseworthy.
If He wills, He will remove you and bring a new creation;
And that is for God not difficult.
And no bearer bears the burden of another. And if one heavy-laden should call to his burden, nothing of it will be carried, though he be a relative. Thou but warnest those who fear their Lord unseen and uphold the duty.

And he who purifies himself: he but purifies himself for
his soul. And to God is the journey's end.
(35:13-18)

Thereupon Zachariah called to his Lord, saying: "My Lord:
give Thou me from Thyself goodly progeny; Thou art
the hearer of supplication."
And the angels called to him as he stood performing the
duty in the chamber: "God gives thee glad tidings of
John, confirming a word from God, both honourable and
chaste, and a prophet among the righteous."
(3:38-39)

Say thou: "Shall we call, rather than to God, to what neither profits us nor harms us, and be turned back on our
heels after God has guided us? — like one whom the
satans seduce in the earth, lost in confusion, he having
companions inviting him to guidance: 'Come thou to
us!'" Say thou: "The guidance of God, that is guidance;
and we have been commanded to submit to the Lord
of All Creation";
And: "Uphold the duty, and be in prudent fear of Him";
and He it is to whom you will be gathered.
(6:71-72)

And We instructed Moses and his brother: "Settle your
people in Egypt in houses, and make your houses a
destination; and uphold the duty; and bear thou glad
tidings to the believers."
And Moses said: "Our Lord: Thou hast given Pharaoh and
his eminent ones adornment and wealth in the life of this
world, our Lord, that they might lead astray from Thy
path. Our Lord: destroy Thou their wealth, and harden
Thou their hearts, so that they believe not until they see
the painful punishment."

He said: "Your supplication has been answered; so take
a straight path, and follow not the path of those who
know not."
(10:87-89)

Say thou: "Call to God, or call to the Almighty; by which-
ever you call, to Him belong the most beautiful names."
And be thou not loud in thy duty, nor quiet therein, but
follow thou a path in-between,
And say thou: "Praise belongs to God who has not taken a
son, and who has no partner in dominion, nor ally from
weakness," and magnify thou Him with glorification.
(17:110-111)

So set thou thy face towards the doctrine, inclining to
truth: — the nature of God with which He created people — (there is no changing the creation of God) that is
the right doctrine, (but most men know not)
Turning in repentance to Him. And be in prudent fear of
Him, and uphold the duty; and be not of the idolaters:
Of those who divide their doctrine and become sects, each
party exulting at what it has.
And when affliction touches men, they call to their Lord,
turning in repentance to Him; then when He lets them
taste mercy from Him, then a faction among them
ascribes a partnership to their Lord,
That they might deny what We have given them. So enjoy
yourselves; and you will come to know!
(30:30-34)

Read the Qur'an

O you who heed warning: approach not the duty when you
are intoxicated until you understand what you say; nor
when you are unclean (save passing by upon the path),
until you wash. And if you were ill, or on a journey, or
one of you comes from the privy, or you have lain with

women, then find not water: resort to clean soil, and wipe your faces and your hands; God is pardoning and forgiving.

Hast thou not considered those given a portion of the Writ, purchasing error and desiring to make you stray from the path?

And God best knows your enemies; and sufficient is God as ally; and sufficient is God as helper.

Some of those who hold to Judaism twist words from their places,[92] — and they say: "We hear and we oppose"; and: "Hear thou what is not heard"; and: "Attend thou to us!" — twisting their tongues, and slandering the doctrine. And had they said: "We hear and we obey"; and: "Hear thou"; and: "Look thou upon us," it would have been better for them, and more upright; but God has cursed them for their denial; and they do not believe save a few.
(4:43-46)

And God took an agreement of the children of Israel; and We raised up among them twelve leaders. And God said: "I am with you if you uphold the duty, and render the purity, and believe in My messengers, and support them, and lend to God a goodly loan. I will remove from you your evil deeds, and make you enter gardens beneath which rivers flow. But whoso among you denies after that has strayed from the right path."

So for their violation of their agreement We cursed them and made their hearts hard. They twist words from their places, and have forgotten a portion of that they were reminded of. And thou wilt not cease to find treachery among them save a few among them; but pardon thou them, and forbear thou; God loves the doers of good.
(5:12-13)

---

92 When they recite the Writ. The duty in this segment is to recite the Writ with careful understanding.

And there followed after them successors who inherited
the Writ, taking the goods of this fleeting life, and saying:
"It will be forgiven us." And if there come to them goods
the like thereof, they will take them. Has there not been
taken from them an agreement to the Writ, that they
ascribe not to God save the truth, and that they study
what is therein? And the abode of the Hereafter is better
for those of prudent fear. Will you then not use reason!
And those who hold fast the Writ, and uphold the duty —
We cause not to be lost the reward of those who do right.
And when We raised the mountain above them as if it were
a canopy: — and they supposed it was to fall upon them
— "Hold fast what We give you; and remember what is
therein, that you might be in prudent fear."
(7:169-171)

Uphold thou the duty at the merging of the sun until the
dark of night, and the recitation of dawn — the recitation
of dawn is witnessed —
And some of the night, keep thou vigil with it, as an addition for thee; it may be that thy Lord will raise thee to
a praised station.
And say thou: "My Lord: cause Thou me to enter at a true
entrance, and to leave at a true exit; and appoint Thou
for me from Thyself a helping authority."
And say thou: "Truth has come, and vanity has passed
away; vanity is to pass away."
(17:78-81)

Those are they whom God favoured among the prophets
of the progeny of Adam, and of those We bore with
Noah, and of the progeny of Abraham and Israel, and
of those We guided and chose. When the proofs of the
Almighty were recited to them, they fell down in submission weeping.
But there succeeded them successors who caused the duty
to be lost, and followed lusts; they will meet with error

Save he who repents and believes and works righteousness, for those will enter the Garden, and they will not
be wronged in anything:
(19:58-60)

Recite thou what has been revealed to thee of the Writ, and
uphold thou the duty; the duty forbids sexual immorality
and perversity; and the remembrance of God is greater;
and God knows what you do.
(29:45)

Those who recite the Writ of God and uphold the duty
and spend of what We have provided them, secretly and
openly, expect a trade that perishes not,
That He will pay their rewards in full, and increase them
out of His bounty; He is forgiving and appreciative.
And that which We revealed to thee of the Writ: it is the
truth, confirming what was before it; God is of His servants aware and seeing.
(35:29-31)

Thy Lord knows that thou standest nearly two-thirds of
the night, or a half of it, or a third of it, as does a number of those with thee. And God determines the night
and the day. He knew that you would not calculate it,
and has turned towards you: — so recite what is made
easy of the Qur'an. He knows that there will be some
sick among you, and others travelling in the earth in
search of the bounty of God, and others fighting in the
cause of God: — so recite what is made easy thereof,
and uphold the duty, and render the purity, and lend
to God a goodly loan. And what good you send ahead
for your souls — you will find it with God, better and
greater in reward. And ask forgiveness of God; God is
forgiving and merciful.
(73:20)

Feed the needy

Hast thou seen him who denies the Doctrine?
That is he who repels the fatherless
And encourages not the feeding of the needy.
Then woe to the performers of duty: —
Those who are of their duty heedless;
Those who make show
And refuse small things!

(107:1-7)

Fight in the cause of God

Had they gone forth with you, they would have increased you only in ruin, and been active in your midst seeking means of denial for you; and among you are eager listeners to them; and God knows the wrongdoers.

They sought the means of denial before, and overturned matters for thee, until the truth came and the command of God was made manifest when they were averse.

And among them is he who says: "Grant thou me leave, and subject thou me not to means of denial." Save into the means of denial have they fallen; and Gehenna encompasses the false claimers of guidance.

If good befalls thee, it vexes them; but if calamity befalls thee, they say: "We took our command before," and they turn away, exulting.

Say thou: "Nothing befalls us save what God has prescribed for us; He is our protector"; and in God let the believers place their trust.

Say thou: "Do you await for us save one of the two best things? And we await for you, that God will afflict you with a punishment from Him or at our hands. So wait — we are with you waiting."

Say thou: "Spend willingly or unwillingly, it will not be accepted from you; you are perfidious people."

And there prevents their expenditures being accepted
from them only that they denied God and His messenger,
and come not to the duty save as idlers, and spend not
save unwillingly.

(9:47-54)

And what you have been given of anything is the enjoyment
of the life of this world; but what is with God is better
and more enduring for those who heed warning and in
their Lord place their trust,

And those who avoid the enormities of sin and sexual
immoralities, and when wroth they forgive,

And those who respond to their Lord, and uphold the duty,
and their affair is by consultation between them, and of
what We have provided them they spend.

And those who, when sectarian zealotry befalls them,
help themselves:

(And the reward of evil is evil the like thereof; but whoso
pardons and makes right, his reward is upon God; He
loves not the wrongdoers.

And whoso helps himself after being wronged, those:
there is no path against them.

There is but a path against those who wrong men and
oppress in the earth without cause: those have a painful
punishment.)

(42:36-42)

Take witnesses when death approaches

O you who heed warning: a witness between you when
death approaches one of you at the time of bequest
is two just men among you; or two others from other
than yourselves if you are travelling in the earth when
the calamity of death befalls you. Detain them after the
duty, and they shall swear by God, if you doubt: "We
would not sell it for a price, though he were a relative,

nor will we conceal the witness of God; then would we
be among the sinners."
(5:106)

The Messenger's duties

And perform thou not the duty for any among them that
dies ever, nor stand thou over his grave; they denied God
and His messenger, and died while they were perfidious.
(9:84)

And among the desert Arabs is he who takes what he
spends as a loss, and awaits reversals for you; for them
is the Evil Reversal; and God is hearing and knowing.
And among the desert Arabs is he who believes in God
and the Last Day, and takes what he spends as a means
of nearness to God and the duties of the Messenger.[93] In
truth, it is a means of nearness for them: God will make
them enter into His mercy; God is forgiving and merciful.
(9:98-99)

Take thou charity of their wealth to cleanse them, and to
increase them in purity thereby; and perform thou the
duty befitting them; thy duties are an assuagement for
them; and God is hearing and knowing.
(9:103)

Help the Messenger

God and His angels perform the duty for the Prophet. O
you who heed warning: perform the duty for him and
greet with a salutation.
Those who hinder God and His messenger: God has cursed
them in the World and the Hereafter, and has prepared
for them a humiliating punishment.

---

93 See 9:103 below.

And those who hinder believing men and believing women with what they have not earned: they bear a calumny and obvious sin.

(33:56-58)

14
GOD'S SERVICE

And I created the domini and the servi only that they
should serve Me.
                    (51:56)

God created man to serve and obey Him alone. The religion of Islam
focuses mostly on ritualistic activities claiming that this is how God has
commanded them to worship Him. However, the Qur'an uses the Arabic
word *abad* to mean both worship and service. Worship of God entails
glorifying and praising Him, asking assistance from Him, thanking Him
and asking forgiveness of Him. Service of God entails obeying Him by
following His commandments in the Qur'an and doing good deeds for
His sake alone. Conversely, to *abad* anyone besides God is to glorify,
thank, ask for assistance or follow others besides Him.

Praising and Glorifying God

In the name of God, the Almighty, the Merciful.
Praise belongs to God, the Lord of All Creation,
The Almighty, the Merciful,
Master of the Day of Judgment.
Thee alone do we serve, and from Thee alone do we seek
    help.
Guide Thou us on the straight path,
The path of those whom Thou hast favoured; not of those
    who incur wrath, nor of those who go astray. (1:1-7)

The essence of worship of God is to call Him by invoking His name, recounting His attributes of Almightiness and Mercy, glorifying Him, testifying to His rightful status as the Lord of all Being, recounting His attributes once again and, finally, testifying to His dominion on the Day, when every soul will be rewarded for what it did.

Calling God alone

Say thou: "Have you considered: if the punishment of God comes upon you, or the Hour comes upon you, will you call to other than God, if you be truthful?"
The truth is, to Him will you call; and He will remove that for which you call to Him if He wills; and you will forget that to which you ascribe a partnership.
(6:40-41)

He it is that lets you travel in the earth and the sea; when you have boarded ships and sailed by them with a good breeze and exulted thereat–– A tempest wind came upon them, and the waves came on them from every side, and they thought they were encompassed therein; they called to God, sincere to Him in doctrine: "If Thou deliver us from this, we will be among the grateful!"
Then when He delivers them, they rebel in the earth without cause.) O mankind: your sectarian zealotry is but against yourselves, — the enjoyment of the life of this world — then to Us is your return and We will inform you of what you did.
(10:22-23)

Say thou: "My Lord has enjoined equity. Uphold your countenances at every place of worship, and call to Him, sincere to Him in doctrine; as He created you, so you will return."
A faction He guided, and upon a faction was misguidance due: they took the satans as allies instead of God, and think they are guided. (7:29-30)

1

So call to God, sincere to Him in doctrine, though the false
claimers of guidance be averse.)
(40:14)

He is the Living; there is no god save He. So call to Him,
sincere to Him in doctrine. Praise belongs to God, the
Lord of All Creation!
(40:65)

Say thou: "O mankind: if you are in doubt about my doctrine: I serve not those whom you serve besides God;
but I serve God, who will take you; and I am commanded
to be of the believers;
"And: 'Set thou thy face towards the doctrine, inclining to
truth; and be thou not of the idolaters;
"'And call thou not, besides God, to what neither profits
thee nor harms thee; for if thou dost, then art thou of
the wrongdoers.'"
And if God should touch thee with affliction, then is there
none to remove it save He; and if He should desire good
for thee, then is there none to repel His bounty: He
causes it to fall upon whom He wills of His servants;
and He is the Forgiving, the Merciful.
(10:104-107)

Glorify, thank and ask forgiveness of God

And We know that thy breast is straitened by what they say.
But give thou glory with the praise of thy Lord, and be
thou among those who submit,
And serve thou thy Lord until the Certainty comes to thee.
(15:97-99)

O you who heed warning: eat of the good things that We
have provided you; and be grateful to God if it be Him
you serve.
(2:172)

So eat of what God has provided you, lawful and good;
and be grateful for the favour of your Lord if it be Him
you serve.

(16:114)

And of His proofs are the night and the day, and the sun
and the moon. Submit not to the sun or the moon, but
submit to God who created them, if it be Him you serve.
But if they have waxed proud, then do those who are with
thy Lord give glory to Him night and day, and they grow
not weary.

(41:37-38)

But submit to God, and serve.

(53:62)

Say thou: "I am forbidden to serve that to which you call
besides God, since there have come to me clear signs
from my Lord; and I am commanded to submit to the
Lord of All Creation."

(40:66)

Do not serve others

And recite thou to them the report of Abraham
When he said to his father and his people: "What do you
serve?"
They said: "We serve idols, and remain to them devoted."
He said: "Do they hear you when you call,
"Or benefit you, or do harm?"
They said: "Nay — we found our fathers doing thus."

(26:69-74)

And it will be said to them: "Where is what you served,
"Besides God? Do they help you, or help themselves?"

(26:92-93)

Say thou: "I have been forbidden to serve those to whom you call besides God." Say thou: "I do not follow your vain desires, else had I gone astray, and would not be of the guided."

(6:56)

Do not serve Satan

And among men is he who serves God upon an edge: if good befalls him he is assuaged thereby, but if a means of denial befalls him he makes an about-face; he has lost the World and the Hereafter. That is the clear loss.
He calls, besides God, to that which neither harms him nor benefits him. That is the extreme error.
He calls to him whose harm is nearer than his benefit. Evil is the protector! And evil is the associate!

(22:11-13)

And the day He gathers them all together, then will He say to the angels: "Did these serve you?"
They will say: "Glory be to Thee! Thou art our ally, not them!" The truth is, they served the domini; most of them were believers in them.
And that day will you possess for one another neither benefit nor harm, and We will say to those who did wrong: "Taste the punishment of the Fire which you denied!"
(34:40-42)

"But separate yourselves this day, O you lawbreakers!
"Did I not commission you, O children of Adam, that you serve not the satan," — he is an open enemy to you —
"But that you serve Me? This is a straight path.
"And he led astray among you a great multitude. Did you then not use reason?

(36:59-62)

"Gather those who did wrong, and their wives, and what
  they served
"Instead of God, and guide them to the path of Hell!
"But stop them — they are to be questioned:
"What ails you that you help not one another?"
The truth is they, this day, are in submission!
And they will draw near to one another, asking one of
  another,
They will say: "You came to us from the right hand[...]."
Those will say: "Nay, you were not believers,
"And we had over you no authority. The truth is, you were
  people transgressing all bounds,
"So the word of our Lord has become binding upon us:
  We are to taste[...].
"And we caused you to err — we were those who err."
                    (37:22-32)

And Hell will be made manifest to those who err,
And it will be said to them: "Where is what you served,
"Besides God? Do they help you, or help themselves?"
And they will be hurled therein, they and those who err,
And the forces of Iblīs all together.
They will say while they dispute therein:
"By God, we were in manifest error
"When we made you equal with the Lord of All Creation!
"And none but the lawbreakers led us astray,
"So now we have no intercessors,
"Nor sincere loyal friend.
"Would that we might return and be among the believers!"
                    (26:91-102)

Serving God includes both worshipping God and obeying His commandments. In the religion of Islam, all emphasis is placed on the
performance of a specific ritual prayer while God's commandments
are — for the most part — ignored.

Say thou: "Shall We inform you of the greatest losers in
deeds?

"Those whose effort is astray in the life of this world when
they think that they are doing good work;

"Those are they who deny the proofs of their Lord and the
meeting with Him; so their works are in vain, and We
will assign to them on the Day of Resurrection no weight.

"That is their reward — Gehenna — because they denied
and took Our proofs and Our messengers in mockery.

"Those who heed warning and do righteous deeds, they
have the Gardens of Paradise as a welcome,

"They abiding eternally therein. They will not desire any
change therefrom."

(18:103-108)

It is not virtue that you turn your faces towards the East
and the West. But virtue is: one who believes in God,
and the Last Day, and the angels, and the Writ, and the
prophets, and gives wealth in spite of love of it to relatives, and the fatherless, and the needy, and the wayfarer,
and those who ask, and to manumit slaves; and who
upholds the duty, and renders the purity; and those
who keep their covenant when they make a covenant;
and the patient in affliction and adversity, and during
conflict: those are they who are sincere; and it is they
who are those of prudent fear.

(2:177)

They believe in God and the Last Day, and enjoin what
is fitting, and forbid perversity, and compete in good
deeds; and those are among the righteous.

(3:114)

And He it is that created the heavens and the earth in six
days, — and His Throne was upon the water — that He
might try you, which of you is best in deed. And if thou

sayest: "You will be raised up after death," those who
ignore warning will say: "This is only obvious sorcery."
(11:7)

We made what is upon the earth an adornment for it,
  that We might try them, which of them is best in deed.
And We will make what is thereon barren ground.
(18:7-8)

In that are proofs; and We are testing.
(23:30)

And We created not the heaven and the earth and what is
  between them to no purpose. That is the assumption of
  those who ignore warning. And woe to those who ignore
  warning from the Fire!
If We make those who heed warning and do righteous
  deeds like the workers of corruption in the land:[...]. — Or
  if We make those of prudent fear like the licentious:[...].
(38:27-28)

15

GLORY OF GOD

God is our only Ally and Protector in this life and the next. The things we value in this life and think will help us, such as wealth, children, and status, will eventually forsake us. God is the only Everlasting Refuge.

> And call thou not with God to another god; there is no god
> save He. Everything will perish save His face; His is the
> Judgment; and to Him will you be returned.
> (28:88)

Let us contemplate the majesty of God. All praise belongs to the Almighty who is not begotten nor has begotten. He does not have any partner in His dominion. The command is His. When He wills a thing to be then it is. God always achieves his command. He knows everything, while we can only know of Him what He wills. Everything in the heavens and the earth obeys and fears Him. The thunder glorifies Him, as do the angels. The heavens are almost rent asunder from fear of Him. We have besides Him no protector or ally. He is perfect in all His attributes. He is the Omnipotent and the Merciful. He bestows His bounty upon whom He wills. He leads astray and guides whom He wills. He is the architect of all things. He has created everything in balance and harmony. There is nothing like Him. He is the Exalter and the Abaser. He is the Severe in Punishment. Judgment is his. He does what He wills. He sustains all creation. He knows all things. In truth, He is the exalted King and all glory is due to Him alone. He is the best of judges and the mightiest of allies. He is the most merciful of those who show mercy and He is the best of those who forgive.

> Knowest thou not that God, to Him belongs the dominion of the heavens and the earth? And you have, besides God, neither ally nor helper.
> (2:107)

> And to God belong the East and the West: wheresoever you turn, there is the face of God; God is encompassing and knowing.
> (2:115)

> God, there is no god save He, the Living, the Eternal. Neither slumber nor sleep overtakes Him; to Him belongs what is in the heavens and what is in the earth — who will intercede with Him save by His leave? He knows what is before them and what is after them, and they encompass not anything of His knowledge save what He wills. His Throne overspreads the heavens and the earth, and the preservation thereof wearies Him not; and He is the Exalted, the Great.
> (2:255)

> To God belongs the dominion of the heavens and the earth and what is in them; and He is over all things powerful.
> (5:120)

> And He is God in the heavens and in the earth; He knows your inward and your outward; and He knows what you earn.
> (6:3)

> And with Him are the keys of the Unseen; and none knows them but He. And He knows what is in the land and the sea; and not a leaf falls but He knows it; nor is there a

grain in the darknesses of the earth, and nothing moist
or dry, but is in a clear writ.

And He it is that takes you at night, and knows what you
earned by day; then He raises you up therein that there
be fulfilled a stated term; then to Him will be your return;
then will He inform you of what you did.

(6:59-60)

And He it is that created the heavens and the earth in truth.
And the day He says: "Be thou," then it is. His word is
the truth. And to Him belongs the dominion the day the
Trumpet is blown — the Knower of the Unseen and the
Seen — and He is the Wise, the Aware.

(6:73)

Vision comprehends Him not, but He comprehends vision;
He is the Subtle, the Aware.

(6:103)

And when Moses came at Our appointed time and his
Lord spoke to him, he said: "My Lord: show Thou me
that I might look upon Thee." Said He: "Thou wilt not
see Me; but look thou upon the mountain: if it should
remain in its place, then thou wilt see Me." And when
his Lord was revealed upon the mountain, He made it
level; and Moses fell down thunderstruck. Then when
he recovered, he said: "Glory be to Thee! I turn to Thee
repentant; and I am the first of the believers!"

(7:143)

And to God submits whoso is in the heavens and the
earth, willingly or unwillingly, as do their shadows in
the mornings and the evenings.

(13:15)

Have they not considered that We come to the earth,
diminishing it from its extremities? And God judges;

there is no adjuster of His judgment; and He is swift in
reckoning.

(13:41)

And to God submits what is in the heavens and what is
in the earth, among creatures and the angels. And they
wax not proud;
They fear their Lord above them, and do what they are
commanded.

(16:49-50)

The seven heavens and the earth and whoso is in them
glorify Him; nothing is save that gives glory with His
praise, but you understand not their glorification; He
is clement and forgiving.

(17:44)

Your God is but God. There is no god save He. He encompasses all things in knowledge.

(20:98)

And to Him belongs whoso is in the heavens and the
earth; and those in His presence are not too proud for
His service, nor do they grow weary,
They give glory night and day, and they flag not.

(21:19-20)

He is not questioned about what He does, but they will
be questioned.

(21:23)

Then exalted be God, the True King! There is no god save
He: the Lord of the Noble Throne.

(23:116)

God is the light of the heavens and the earth. The likeness
of His light is as a niche wherein is a lamp — the lamp

in a glass, the glass as it were a shining star — lit from
a blessed tree, an olive neither of East nor West; its oil
would nigh illuminate, though no fire touched it: — light
upon light! — God guides to His light whom He wills!
And God strikes similitudes for men; and God knows
all things.

(24:35)

Dost thou not see that God, to Him gives glory whoso is
in the heavens and the earth, and the birds with wings
outstretched? Each, he knows his duty and his glorification; and God knows what they do.
And to God belongs the dominion of the heavens and the
earth; and to God is the journey's end.

(24:41-42)

And call thou not with God to another god; there is no god
save He. Everything will perish save His face; His is the
Judgment; and to Him will you be returned.

(28:88)

God holds the heavens and the earth lest they cease. And
if they should cease, no one could hold them after Him.
He is clement and forgiving.

(35:41)

His command, when He intends a thing, is that He says to
it: "Be thou," and it is.
So glory be to Him in whose hand is the dominion of all
things! And to Him you will be returned.

(36:82-83)

And they measured God not with the measure due Him.
And the earth altogether will be His handful on the Day
of Resurrection, and the heavens will be folded up in His
right hand. Glory be to Him! And exalted is He above that
to which they ascribe a partnership! (39:67)

And Our command is but one — as the twinkling of an
eye[...].

(54:50)

Everyone on it[94] is to perish,
But the face of thy Lord will remain, Owner of Majesty
and Honour.

(55:26-27)

What is in the heavens and the earth gives glory to God;
and He is the Exalted in Might, the Wise.

(57:1)

Blessed be He in whose hand is the dominion — and He
is over all things powerful —

(67:1)

Be you secret in your speech or proclaim it, He knows
that which is in the breasts.
Should He not know, He who created? And He is the Subtle, the Aware.

(67:13-14)

Have they not seen the birds above them with wings
outstretched and closing? None holds them but the
Almighty. He sees all things.

(67:19)

The might of thy Lord is strong.
He is it who originates, and He repeats.
And He is the Forgiving, the Loving,
Owner of the Throne, the Glorious,
Doer of what He intends.

(85:12-16)

---

94 i.e. the earth.

Attributes of God

Lord of the Daybreaks
Lord of the Noble Throne
Lord of the Seven Heavens
Lord of the Tremendous Throne
Master of Dominion
Master of the Day of Judgment
Owner of the Means of Ascent
The Absolute
The Ally
The Almighty
The Appreciative
The Aware
The Benefactor
The Bestower
The Compeller
The Creating
The Creator
The Eternal
The Exalted
The Faithful
The Fashioner
The First
The Forbearing
The Forgiving
The Free from Need
The Great
The Guardian
The Hearing
The Holy
The Inner
The King
The Knowing
The Knowing Creator
The Knowing Judge
The Last

The Living
The Lord of All Mankind
The Lord of Firm Might
The Lord of Greatness
The Lord of Sirius
The Lord of the Earth
The Lord of the Easts and the Wests
The Lord of the Heavens
The Lord of the Heavens and the Earth
The Lord of the Heavens and the Earth and what is
  between them
The Lord of the Noble Throne
The Lord of the Sky and the Earth
The Lord of the Throne
The Lord of the Two Easts
The Lord of the Two Wests
The Loving
The Merciful
The Mighty
The Most High
The Noble
The Omnipotent
The One
The Originator
The Outer
The Owner of Abundance
The Owner of Majesty and Honor
The Owner of the Glorious Throne
The Owner of the Throne
The Pardoning
The Perfect
The Possessor of Mercy
The Praiseworthy
The Preserver
The Provider
The Quickener of the Dead
The Raiser of Degrees

The Receptive
The Seeing
The Strong
The Subtle
The Supreme
The Tremendous
The Truth
The Virtuous
The Wise

16
REALITY OF
THIS LIFE

The life of this life is a fleeting pleasure punctuated with a lot of pain. We are born, we live, and we die. People distract themselves endlessly to forget this reality, but sooner or later death catches up to them. There is no escape.

> Say thou: "If the abode of the Hereafter with God be for you to the exclusion of other men, then wish for death, if you be truthful."
> But never will they wish for it because of what their hands have sent ahead; and God knows the wrongdoers.
> And thou wilt find them the greediest of men for life. And of those who ascribe a partnership: one of them wishes to be granted life of a thousand years, but it will not remove him from the punishment were he to be granted life; and God sees what they do.
> (2:94-96)

> Every soul will taste death; and you will but be paid in full your rewards on the Day of Resurrection. And whoso is removed from the Fire and made to enter the Garden: he has attained; and the life of this world is only the enjoyment of delusion. (3:185)

Wherever you be, death will overtake you, though you be in castles built high. And if good befalls them, they say: "This is from God"; and if evil befalls them, they say: "This is from thee." Say thou: "All is from God." Then what ails these people that they scarcely understand a statement?

(4:78)

Have they not reflected? Their companion is not possessed; he is only a clear warner.
Have they not considered the dominion of the heavens and the earth, and what things God has created, and that it may be that their term has drawn nigh? And in what narration after this will they believe?

(7:184-185)

The likeness of the life of this world is but like water We send down from the sky, and the plants of the earth mingle with it, whereof men and cattle eat: when the earth has taken her decoration, and is made fair, and its people think they have power over it, Our command comes by night or by day, and We make it reaped as if it had not flourished the day before — thus do We set out and detail the proofs for people who reflect.

(10:24)

And strike thou for them the similitude of the life of this world: — as water which We send down from the sky, then the vegetation of the earth mingles with it; then it becomes dry stalks which the winds scatter. And God is omnipotent over everything.

(18:45)

We will inherit the earth and whoso is thereon, and to Us will they be returned.

(19:40)

They know an outward part of the life of this world, but
   of the Hereafter they are heedless.
(30:7)

Know that the life of this world is only play and diversion,
   and adornment, and mutual boasting among you, and
   competition for increase in wealth and children. As
   the likeness of a rain, it impresses the atheists with its
   growth; then it withers and thou seest it turn yellow;
   then it becomes debris. And in the Hereafter is severe
   punishment, and forgiveness from God, and approval.
   And the life of this world is only the enjoyment of
   delusion.
(57:20)

Glorify thou the name of thy Lord, the Most High,
Who created and fashioned,
And who determined and guided,
And who brought forth the pasture
Then made it blackening decaying herbage
(87:1-5)

The truth is, you prefer the life of this world
When the Hereafter is better and more enduring.
(87:16-17)

Ancient Civilizations

How many great civilizations have gone before us? All former civilizations have been destroyed by God due to their transgressions. The same
fate awaits the current scientific tyranny[95] that we are living under.

And there is no city save We will destroy it before the Day
   of Resurrection, or punish it with severe punishment;
   that is in the Writ inscribed.
(17:58)

---

95 See my book *Tyranny2.0* for details.

God destroys a civilization when it reaches the pinnacle of its decadence, immorality and transgression. He is watching over His servants and allows the wicked time to work corruption in the land. But when their term ends, God is swift in reckoning.

> Have they not considered how many a generation We
> destroyed before them? We established them in the earth
> as We have not established you, and We sent the sky
> upon them in abundant rains and made the rivers flow
> beneath them; then We destroyed them for their trans-
> gressions, and produced after them another generation.
> (6:6)

> Say thou: "Travel in the earth, then see how was the final
> outcome of the deniers."
> (6:11)

> Say thou: "Look at what is in the heavens and the earth!"
> But the proofs and the warnings avail not a people who
> do not believe.
> Do they await save the like of the days of those who passed
> away before them? Say thou: "Then wait — I am with
> you waiting."
> (10:101-102)

> And We sent before thee only men to whom We revealed
> from among the people of the cities. (So have they not
> travelled in the earth and seen how was the final out-
> come of those who were before them? And the abode of
> the Hereafter is best for those who are in prudent fear;
> will you then not use reason!)
> (12:109)

> And when Our proofs are recited to them as clear signs,
> those who ignore warning say to those who heed warn-
> ing: "Which of the two factions is better in standing and
> better in assembly?"

But how many a generation We destroyed before
them which was better in possessions and outward
appearance!
(19:73-74)

And how many a generation We destroyed before them!
Perceivest thou any one of them, or hearest thou from
them a sound?
(19:98)

Does it not then guide them how many generations We
destroyed before them in whose dwellings they walk?
In that are proofs for possessors of intelligence.
(20:128)

"But," — they say — "a confused medley of dreams; but
he has invented it; but he is a poet. So let him bring us
a proof like that sent to the former peoples!"
No city believed before them among those We destroyed;
will they then believe?
And We sent before thee only men to whom We revealed
— and ask the people of the remembrance, if you know
not —
(21:5-7)

And We created not the heaven and the earth and what
is between them in play.
Had We wished to take a diversion, We would have taken
it from Ourselves — if We are the doers.
(21:16-17)

And how many a city did We destroy when it was doing
wrong and is desolate! — and a deserted well[...]! and
a lofty castle[...]!
(Have they not travelled in the earth and had hearts with
which to reason, or ears with which to hear? And it is not

the eyes that are blind, but blind are the hearts which are in the breasts.

And they ask thee to hasten the punishment! But God does not fail in His promise. And a day with thy Lord is as a thousand years of what you count.)

(22:45-47)

And those who ignore warning say: "When we are dust, and our fathers, will we be brought forth?

"We have been promised this, we and our fathers, before; this is only legends of the former peoples."

Say thou: "Travel in the earth and see how was the final outcome of the lawbreakers." (27:67-69)

And how many a city We destroyed that was insolent in its livelihood; and those are their dwellings: they have not been inhabited after them save a little. And We are the inheritors.

(28:58)

Have they not travelled in the earth and seen how was the final outcome of those who were before them? They were stronger than them in power, and they tilled the earth and inhabited it more than they have inhabited it; and their messengers came to them with clear signs; and God wronged them not, but they wronged their souls.

(30:9)

Say thou: "Travel in the earth and see how was the final outcome of those who were before; most of them were idolaters."

(30:42)

Does it not guide them, how many generations We destroyed before them among whose dwellings they walk? In that are proofs. Will they then not hear!

(32:26)

Have they not travelled in the earth and seen how was
the final outcome of those who were before them? And
they were stronger than them in power; but God is not
such that anything in the heavens or in the earth should
frustrate Him; He is knowing and powerful.
(35:44)

Have they not considered how many generations We
destroyed before them — that they to them will not
return?
And all of them will be brought present before Us.
(36:31-32)

Have they not travelled in the earth and seen how was
the final outcome of those before them? They were
more numerous than they, and stronger in power and
impact in the earth; but there availed them not what
they earned.
When their messengers came to them with clear signs,
they exulted at what they had of knowledge; but there
surrounded them that whereat they mocked.
(40:82-83)

Then as for 'Ād: they had waxed proud in the land without cause, and they said: "Who is stronger than us in
power?" Had they not considered that God who created
them, He was stronger than them in power? And they
rejected Our proofs.
(41:15)

And We destroyed stronger than them in might; and the
example of the former peoples has gone before.
(43:8)

And We have destroyed what surrounds you of cities;
and We expounded the proofs, that they might return.
(46:27)

Have they not travelled in the earth and seen how was
the final outcome of those who were before them? God
destroyed them; and for the false claimers of guidance
are the likes thereof

For it is that God is the protector of those who heed warning, and that the false claimers of guidance have no
protector!

(47:10-11)

And how many a generation We destroyed before them
stronger than them in might! And they penetrated into
the land; had they any place of refuge? (50:36)

Did We not destroy the former peoples?

Then will We cause to follow them those who come later.

(77:16-17)

17
WARNING

The truth is, those who do wrong follow their vain desires
without knowledge; then who will guide him whom God
has sent astray? And they have no helpers.
So set thou thy face towards the doctrine, inclining to
truth: — the nature of God with which He created people — (there is no changing the creation of God) that is
the right doctrine, (but most men know not)
Turning in repentance to Him. And be in prudent fear of
Him, and uphold the duty; and be not of the idolaters:
Of those who divide their doctrine and become sects, each
party exulting at what it has.
(30:29-32)

Some men intuit a purpose to their creation. They know that they
must take the steep path towards self-purification, but they delay and
make excuses. We need to understand the urgency of the matter; the
Day of Judgment is near. Be not one of those who put off action and be
full of regrets on the Day. God has proclaimed that He will not change
the condition of a people until they change what is within themselves.

He has successive angels before him and after him, keeping
him by the command of God. God changes not what is in
a people until they change what is in themselves. And
when God intends evil for a people, there is no repelling
it; and they have besides Him no ally. (13:11)

If you desire right guidance then I implore you to not put off the matter any longer. Begin by repenting sincerely to God and admit your transgressions. Ask God for guidance and read the Qur'an. It alone is the source of guidance. It would be sheer folly to forsake such an incredible gift from God and remain ignorant of its teachings.

> This Qur'an guides to what is most upright, and brings
>   glad tidings to the believers who do righteous deeds,
>   that they have a great reward,
> And that those who believe not in the Hereafter: — We
>   have prepared for them a painful punishment.
> (17:9-10)

> And be in prudent fear of a day no soul will avail a soul
>   anything, nor will intercession be accepted from it,
>   nor will compensation be taken from it; nor will they
>   be helped.
> (2:48)

> What proof We abolish or cause to be forgotten, We bring
>   one better than it or the like thereof; knowest thou not
>   that God is over all things powerful?
> (2:106)

> Look they save for God to come to them in shadows of the
>   clouds, and the angels? But the matter is concluded, and
>   to God are matters returned.
> (2:210)

> And if thou couldst see when they are set before the Fire:
>   — then they will say: "Would that we were sent back!
>   Then would we not deny the proofs of our Lord, but be
>   among the believers."
> (6:27)

> And if thou couldst see when they are set before their
>   Lord: — He will say: "Is then this not the truth?" They

will say: "Verily, by our Lord!" He will say: "Then taste the punishment for what you denied!"

They have lost who deny the meeting with God; when the Hour has come upon them unexpectedly, they will say: "O our regret over what we neglected concerning it!" And they will bear their burdens upon their backs; in truth, evil is what they will bear.

(6:30-31)

That which you are promised is coming; and you cannot escape.

(6:134)

Look they save for the angels to come to them, or thy Lord to come, or for there to come some of the proofs of thy Lord? The day there come some of the proofs of thy Lord, the faith of a soul will benefit it nothing which had not believed before, nor by its faith earned good. Say thou: "Wait — we are waiting."

(6:158)

They ask thee concerning the Hour: "When is its arrival?" Say thou: "Knowledge thereof is but with my Lord; none reveals its time save He. It weighs heavily in the heavens and the earth; it comes not upon you save unexpectedly." They ask thee as though thou wert privy thereto; say thou: "Knowledge thereof is but with God"; but most men know not.

(7:187)

And the day He gathers them will be as if they had tarried only an hour of the day: they will recognise one another; those will have lost who denied the meeting with God and were not guided.

(10:45)

And think thou not that God is unmindful of what the
wrongdoers do; He only delays them to a day wherein
the eyes will stare,
Straining forward, their heads uplifted; their gaze not
returning to them, and their hearts void.
And warn thou mankind of a day the punishment will come
upon them, and those who did wrong will say: "Our Lord:
delay Thou us for a short term: we will respond to Thy
call and follow the messengers." — "Did you not swear
before that there would be no end for you?
"And you dwelt in the dwellings of those who wronged
their souls; and it was made clear to you how We did
with them; and We struck similitudes for you."
(14:42-45)

And to God belongs the unseen of the heavens and the
earth. And the matter of the Hour is only as the twinkling
of the eye, or even nearer; God is over all things powerful.
(16:77)

And the day We raise up from every community a witness,
then no leave will be given those who ignore warning
nor will they be allowed to make amends.
And when those who do wrong see the punishment, it
will not be lightened for them, nor will they be granted
respite.
(16:84-85)

The day every soul comes pleading for itself, and every
soul is repaid in full for what it did; and they will not
be wronged.
(16:111)

And the day We set in motion the mountains, and thou
seest the earth emerge, and We gather them, then will
We not leave behind one of them

And they will be set before thy Lord in ranks: "You have come to Us as We created you the first time; yet you claimed that We would never make an appointment for you!"

And the writ will be set down, and thou wilt see the law-breakers apprehensive of what is therein. And they will say: "Woe is us! What writ is this that leaves behind nothing small or great save it has enumerated it?" And they will find what they did present; and thy Lord wrongs no one.

(18:47-49)

Then the parties differed among themselves; then woe to those who ignore warning from the meeting of a tremendous day.

How they hear and how they see the day they come to Us! But the wrongdoers are this day in manifest error.

And warn thou them of the Day of Regret, when the matter will be concluded; but they are in heedlessness, and they do not believe.

(19:37-39)

"And let not turn thee away from it him who believes not in it but follows his vain desire, or thou wilt perish.

(20:16)

That day will they follow the Caller having no deviation; and voices will be stilled before the Almighty, and thou wilt hear not save a murmur.

(20:108)

And had We destroyed them with a punishment before him, they would have said: "Our Lord: oh, that Thou hadst but sent to us a messenger, so we might have followed Thy proofs before we were humiliated and disgraced!"

(20:134)

Drawn nigh to men has their reckoning, while they in
heedlessness are turning away;
(21:1)

If those who ignore warning but knew the time when they
will not restrain the Fire from their faces, nor from their
backs, nor will they be helped!
But it will come upon them unexpectedly, and render them
speechless, and they will be unable to repel it, nor will
they be granted respite.
(21:39-40)

And drawn nigh has the true promise; and then the eyes
of those who ignore warning will stare: "Woe is us! We
had been in heedlessness of this. The truth is, we were
wrongdoers."
(21:97)

O mankind: be in prudent fear of your Lord! The convul-
sion of the Hour is a tremendous thing.
The day you see it, every one nursing will neglect what she
suckled, and every one pregnant will deliver her burden,
and thou wilt see mankind intoxicated when they are
not intoxicated; but the punishment of God is severe.
(22:1-2)

And that the Hour about which there is no doubt is coming;
and that God will raise those in the graves!
(22:7)

When death has come to one of them, he says: "My Lord:
send Thou me back,
"That I might work righteousness in what I left behind."
No, indeed! It is but a word that he says; and behind
them is a barrier until the day they are raised.
(23:99-100)

The truth is, they have denied the Hour; and We have
prepared for him who denies the Hour an inferno.
When it[96] sees them from a place far away, they will hear
the fury and the roaring thereof.
And when they are cast therefrom into a narrow place
bound together, they will call thereupon for destruction.
"Call not this day for one destruction, but call for many
destructions!"
(25:11-14)

And the day the Trumpet is blown, then terrified will be
whoso is in the heavens and the earth save who God
wills, and all will come to Him abased.
(27:87)

And were God to take men for what they earn, He would
not leave any creature upon its surface. But He delays
them to a stated term. But when their term comes, then
is God of His servants seeing.
(35:45)

They look only for one Blast which will seize them while
they are disputing —
They will not be able to make a bequest, nor will they
return to their people.
And the Trumpet will be blown; and then from the graves
will they hasten forth to their Lord.
They will say: "Woe is us! Who has raised us from our
sleeping place?" — "This is what the Almighty promised!
And the emissaries spoke truth!"
(36:49-52)

They will have above them canopies of the Fire, and
beneath them canopies. By that does God put His servants in dread: "O My servants: be in prudent fear of Me!"
(39:16)

_____

96 i.e. Hell.

And warn thou them of the Day of the Drawing Near, when
the hearts will choke in the throats: — No loyal friend
for the wrongdoers! No intercessor who is obeyed!
(40:18)

The Hour is coming — about which there is no doubt —
but most men do not believe.
(40:59)

God it is who has sent down the Writ with the truth and
the balance. And what can make thee know that the
Hour might be nigh!
(42:17)

Respond to your Lord before there comes a day there is
no repelling from God; you will have no refuge that day,
nor will there be for you any denial.
(42:47)

Then leave thou them until they meet their day wherein
they will be thunderstruck,
A day in which their plan will avail them nothing, and they
will not be helped.
(52:45-46)

The Drawing Near has drawn near.
(53:57)

The truth is, the Hour is their appointment; and the Hour
is more calamitous and more bitter.
(54:46)

We created everything in measure
And Our command is but one — as the twinkling of an
eye[...].
And We have destroyed your sects before, so is there any
who will remember? (54:49-51)

When the Event befalls,
— There is no denying its befalling —
Abasing, exalting;
(56:1-3)

Then when the Trumpet is blown with a single blast,
And the earth and the mountains are lifted up and levelled
    with a single blow,
Then, that day, the Event will befall,
And the sky be split asunder for it, that day, is frail,
And the angels on its sides; and there will bear the Throne
    of thy Lord above them, that day, eight.
That day, you will be presented; no secret among you will
    be concealed.
(69:13-18)

So leave thou them to discourse vainly and play until they
    meet their day which they are promised:
The day they will come forth from the graves in haste, as
    though towards an idol, running,
Their eyes humbled, humiliation covering them. That is
    the day which they are promised.
(70:42-44)

He asks: "When is the Day of Resurrection?"
Then when the sight is dazzled,
And the moon is eclipsed,
And sun and moon are joined,
Man will say: — that day — "Whither to flee?"
No, indeed! There is no sanctuary.
To thy Lord, that day, is the destination.
Man will be informed, that day, of what he sent before
    and held back.
(75:6-13)

What you are promised — it will befall.
(77:7)

Lord of the Heavens and the Earth and what is between
them, the Almighty. They have from Him no power to
speak

The day the Spirit and the angels stand in ranks; they
speak not save he whom the Almighty grants leave, and
he will say what is right.

That is the True Day, so let him who wills take his Lord
as a journey's end.

We have warned you of a near punishment: the day a man
will look on what his hands sent ahead, and the false
claimer of guidance will say: "Would that I were dust!"
(78:37-40)

It will be, the day they see it, as though they had not tarried
save a day's end or a morning thereof.
(79:46)

Then when there comes the Blast:

The day a man will flee from his brother,

And his mother, and his father,

And his consort, and his sons,

Every man of them, that day, will have an involvement to
suffice him.
(80:33-37)

No, indeed! When the earth is ground to powder,

And thy Lord comes — and the angels, rank upon rank —

And Gehenna, that day, is brought: that day will man take
heed; but how will the reminder be for him?

He will say: "Would that I had sent ahead for my life!"

And — that day — none will punish as His punishment,

And none will bind as His binding.
(89:21-26)

So I have warned you of a raging Fire

In which burns only the most wretched:

Who denied and turned away. (92:14-16)

When the earth is shaken with great shaking,
And the earth brings forth its burdens,
And man says: "What ails it?"
That day, it will recount its news
Because thy Lord has instructed it.
(99:1-5)

The Calamity!
What is the Calamity?
And what will convey to thee what the Calamity is?
The day men will be as moths dispersed,
And the mountains as wool fluffed up.
(101:1-5)

Last Words

"So flee to God! I am to you from Him a clear warner!
(51:50)

And recite thou to them the report of him to whom We
gave Our proofs, but he detached himself from them;
so the satan followed him, and he was of those who err.
And had We willed, We would have raised him thereby;
but he clung to the earth and followed his vain desire.
So his likeness is as the likeness of a dog: if thou win
him over, he pants; or if thou leave him, he pants. That
is the likeness of the people who deny Our proofs; so
relate thou to them the story, that they might reflect.
(7:175-176)

I hope that my presentation of the numerous and diverse arguments of God provide you with an impetus to sincerely and diligently study it[97] and question the beliefs you were born into. Time is short, no man knows where and when he will die. I urge you to not defer this grave matter any longer but to strive with all your might to gain the good pleasure of God. God invites us to ponder His proofs by using our

---

97 I recommend the excellent work : *The Quran: A Complete Revelation*, Sam Gerrans.

reason and thereby come to an unshakable belief in Him. Only then can we every hope to serve the One True God and attain everlasting bliss.

> The worst of beasts in the sight of God are the deaf, the
> dumb — those who do not reason.
>> (8:22)

> "Did I not commission you, O children of Adam, that you
> serve not the satan," — he is an open enemy to you —
> "But that you serve Me? This is a straight path.
> "And he led astray among you a great multitude. Did you
> then not use reason?
> "This is Gehenna: — which you were promised —
> "Burn therein this day, for what you denied!"
>> (36:60-64)

***

> Say thou: "O My servants who have committed excess
> against their souls: despair not of the mercy of God!
> God forgives transgressions altogether, — He is the
> Forgiving, the Merciful —
> "And turn in repentance to your Lord, and submit to Him
> before there comes to you the punishment; then will
> you not be helped."
> And follow the best of what is sent down to you from
> your Lord, before the punishment comes upon you
> unexpectedly when you perceive not
>> (39:53-55)

18

PRAYERS
FROM THE QUR'AN

In the name of God, the Almighty, the Merciful.
Praise belongs to God, the Lord of All Creation,
The Almighty, the Merciful,
Master of the Day of Judgment.
Thee alone do we serve, and from Thee alone do we seek
    help.
Guide Thou us on the straight path,
The path of those whom Thou hast favoured; not of those
    who incur wrath, nor of those who go astray.
(1:1-7)

And among them is he who says: "Our Lord: give Thou
    to us in the World good, and in the Hereafter good, and
    protect Thou us from the punishment of the Fire."
(2:201)

And when they emerged against Goliath and his forces,
    they said: "Our Lord: pour Thou out patience upon us,
    and make Thou firm our feet; and help Thou us against
    the people of the false claimers of guidance."
(2:250)

God burdens not a soul save to its capacity; it has what it earned, and it answers for what it acquired. "Our Lord: take Thou us not to task if we forget or commit offence. Our Lord: lay Thou not upon us a burden as Thou didst lay upon those before us. Our Lord: give Thou us not to bear what we have not strength for. And excuse Thou us, and forgive Thou us, and have Thou mercy upon us; Thou art our protector. And help Thou us against the people of the false claimers of guidance."
(2:286)

He it is that sent down upon thee the Writ; among it are explicit proofs: they are the foundation of the Writ; and others are ambiguous. Then as for those in whose hearts is deviation: they follow what is ambiguous thereof, seeking the means of denial, and seeking its interpretation. And no one knows its interpretation save God, and those firm in knowledge; they say: "We believe in it; all is from our Lord." But only those of insight take heed.
"Our Lord: make Thou not our hearts to deviate after Thou hast guided us; and bestow Thou upon us mercy from Thyself; Thou art the Bestower.
"Our Lord: Thou art gathering mankind to a day about which there is no doubt"; God will not break the appointment.
(3:7-9)

Say thou: "O God, Master of Dominion: Thou givest dominion to whom Thou wilt, and Thou removest dominion from whom Thou wilt; Thou exaltest whom Thou wilt, and Thou abasest whom Thou wilt. In Thy hand is good; Thou art over all things powerful.
"Thou makest the night enter into the day, and Thou makest the day enter into the night; and Thou bringest forth the living from the dead, and Thou bringest forth the dead from the living. And Thou givest provision to whom Thou wilt without reckoning." (3:26-27)

Thereupon Zachariah called to his Lord, saying: "My Lord: give Thou me from Thyself goodly progeny; Thou art the hearer of supplication."

(3:38)

And those who, when they commit sexual immorality or wrong their souls, remember God, and ask forgiveness for their transgressions — and who forgives transgressions save God? — and persist not in what they did when they know.

(3:135)

And their word was only that they said: "Our Lord: forgive Thou us our transgressions, and our excess in our affair, and make Thou firm our feet; and help Thou us against the people of the false claimers of guidance."

(3:147)

Those who remember God, standing and sitting and on their sides, and reflect upon the creation of the heavens and the earth: "Our Lord: Thou createdst not this to no purpose. Glory be to Thee! And protect Thou us from the punishment of the Fire!

"Our Lord: whom Thou causest to enter the Fire: him hast Thou disgraced"; and there are for the wrongdoers no helpers.

"Our Lord: we have heard a caller calling to faith: 'Believe in your Lord!' And we have believed. Our Lord: forgive Thou us our transgressions, and remove Thou from us our evil deeds; and take Thou us with the virtuous.

"Our Lord: give Thou us what Thou hast promised us by Thy messengers, and disgrace Thou us not on the Day of Resurrection; Thou wilt not break the appointment."

(3:191-194)

Say thou: "Who delivers you from the darknesses of the
land and the sea? You call to Him humbly and in secret: 'If
He delivers us from this, we will be among the grateful.'"
(6:63)

They said: "Our Lord: we have wronged our souls; and if
Thou forgive us not and have not mercy on us, we will
be among the losers."
(7:23)

And when their eyes are turned towards the companions
of the Fire, they say: "Our Lord: place Thou not us with
the wrongdoing people."
(7:47)

They said: "We are returning to our Lord.
"And thou resentest us only that we believed in the proofs
of our Lord when they came to us." — "Our Lord: pour
Thou out patience upon us, and take Thou us as ones
submitting."
(7:125-126)

And when Moses came at Our appointed time and his
Lord spoke to him, he said: "My Lord: show Thou me
that I might look upon Thee." Said He: "Thou wilt not
see Me; but look thou upon the mountain: if it should
remain in its place, then thou wilt see Me." And when
his Lord was revealed upon the mountain, He made it
level; and Moses fell down thunderstruck. Then when
he recovered, he said: "Glory be to Thee! I turn to Thee
repentant; and I am the first of the believers!"
(7:143)

He said: "My Lord: forgive Thou me and my brother, and
enter Thou us into Thy mercy; and Thou art the most
merciful of those who show mercy."
(7:151)

And Moses chose of his people seventy men for Our appointed time; then when the earthquake seized them, he said: "My Lord: if Thou hadst willed, Thou wouldst have destroyed them before, and me. Wilt Thou destroy us for what the foolish among us have done? It is but Thy means of denial: Thou sendest whom Thou wilt astray thereby, and guidest whom Thou wilt. Thou art our ally, so forgive Thou us, and have Thou mercy on us; and Thou art the best of those who forgive.

"And prescribe Thou for us in the World good, and in the Hereafter; we have returned to Thee." He said: "I strike with My punishment whom I will; but My mercy encompasses all things: I will ordain it for those of prudent fear, and who render the purity, and those who believe in Our proofs:

(7:155-156)

Then if they turn away, say thou: "God is sufficient for me; there is no god save He. In Him have I placed my trust, and He is Lord of the Great Throne."

(9:129)

And Moses said: "O my people: if you believe in God, then place your trust in Him, if you are submitting."

And they said: "In God have we placed our trust." — "Our Lord: make Thou not us a means of denial for the wrongdoing people,

"And deliver Thou us by Thy mercy from the people of the false claimers of guidance."

(10:84-86)

And Noah called to his Lord, and said: "My Lord: my son was of my household — and Thy promise is the truth; and Thou art the most just of judges."

He said: "O Noah: he was not of thy household. He was a deed not righteous; so ask thou Me not of that whereof thou hast no knowledge; I admonish thee lest thou be of the ignorant."

Said he: "My Lord, in Thee do I seek refuge lest I ask of Thee that whereof I have no knowledge; and save Thou forgive me, and have mercy on me, I will be among the losers."

(11:45-47)

"My Lord: Thou hast given me some dominion, and hast taught me some of the interpretation of events; Creator of the Heavens and the Earth: Thou art my ally in the World and the Hereafter. Take Thou me as one submitting, and join Thou me with the righteous."

(12:101)

"Praise belongs to God who has given me in old age Ishmael and Isaac! My Lord is the hearer of supplication.

"My Lord: make Thou me one upholding the duty, and of my progeny, our Lord, and accept Thou my supplication.

"Our Lord: forgive Thou me, and my parents, and the believers, the day the reckoning takes place.")

(14:39-41)

And lower thou to them the wing of gentleness out of mercy, and say thou: "My Lord: have mercy on them, as they brought me up when I was small."

(17:24)

And say thou: "Praise belongs to God who has not taken a son, and who has no partner in dominion, nor ally from weakness," and magnify thou Him with glorification.

(17:111)

And say thou: "My Lord: cause Thou me to enter at a true entrance, and to leave at a true exit; and appoint Thou for me from Thyself a helping authority."

And say thou: "Truth has come, and vanity has passed
away; vanity is to pass away."
(17:80-81)

(When the young men took shelter in the cave and said:
"Our Lord: give Thou us mercy from Thyself, and furnish
Thou us out of our affair with rectitude,"
(18:10)

"But I fear my heirs after me, and my wife is barren, so
give Thou me from Thyself an heir
(19:5)

Said he: "My Lord: expand Thou for me my breast,
"And ease Thou for me my affair,
"And loosen Thou the knot from my tongue,
"That they might understand my speech.
"And appoint Thou for me an assistant from my family:
"Aaron, my brother;
"Strengthen Thou by him my strength,
"And make Thou him share in my affair,
"That we might glorify Thee much,
"And remember Thee much.
"Thou dost see us."
(20:25-35)

And exalted be God, the True King! And hasten thou not
with the recitation before its revelation to thee be complete; and say thou: "My Lord: increase Thou me in
knowledge."
(20:114)

And Job: when he called to his Lord: "Adversity has touched
me, and Thou art the most merciful of those who show
mercy,"
(21:83)

And Dhūl-Nūn: when he left in wrath, and thought that
   We would have no power over him; then he called in
   the darkness: "There is no god save Thou. Glory be to
   Thee! I have been among the wrongdoers!"
(21:87)

And Zachariah: when he called to his Lord: "My Lord:
   leave Thou me not solitary; and Thou art the best of
   inheritors,"
(21:89)

Say thou: "My Lord: judge Thou with justice. And our Lord
   is the Almighty, the one whose aid is sought against
   what you describe."
(21:112)

He said: "My Lord: help Thou me because they have denied
   me."
And We instructed him: "Make thou the ship under Our
   eyes and Our instruction; then when Our command
   comes and the oven boils over, load thou therein of each
   kind two, and thy household save him against whom
   the word has gone forth among them. And address thou
   Me not on behalf of those who do wrong; they will be
   drowned.
"And when thou art seated — thou and whoso is with
   thee — upon the ship, say thou: 'Praise belongs to God
   who has delivered us from the wrongdoing people.'"
"And say thou: 'My Lord: set Thou me down at a blessed
   landing-place; and Thou art the best of those who set
   down.'"
(23:26-29)

Say thou: "My Lord: if Thou show me what they are
   promised,
"My Lord: then place Thou me not among the wrongdoing
   people." (23:93-94)

And say thou: "My Lord: forgive Thou, and have Thou
mercy; and Thou art the best of those who have mercy."
(23:118)

And who say: "Our Lord: avert Thou from us the punishment of Gehenna"; (the punishment thereof is
unrelenting,
Evil is it as a dwelling-place and a residence)
(25:65-66)

And who say: "Our Lord: give Thou to us from our wives
and our progeny a comfort of the eyes, and make Thou
us a model for those of prudent fear,"
(25:74)

"My Lord: give Thou me judgment, and join Thou me with
the righteous,
"And appoint Thou for me a tongue of truth among those
who come later.
"And make Thou me among the inheritors of the Garden
of Bliss.
"And forgive Thou my father; he is of those who go astray.
"And disgrace Thou me not the day they are raised:
"The day wealth and sons benefit not
"Save him who comes to God with a pure heart."
(26:83-89)

He said: "My Lord: my people have denied me,
"So decide Thou between me and them, and deliver Thou
me and those with me among the believers."
(26:117-118)

And he smiled, laughing at her speech, and he said: "My
Lord: direct Thou me to be grateful for Thy favour wherewith Thou favoured me and my parents, and to work
righteousness pleasing to Thee; and make Thou me enter,
by Thy mercy, among Thy righteous servants." (27:19)

He said: "My Lord: I have wronged my soul; so forgive
Thou me," and He forgave him; He is the Forgiving, the
Merciful.
He said: "My Lord: for that which Thou hast favoured me,
nevermore will I be helper to the lawbreakers."
(28:16-17)

And he went out therefrom in dread, expectant. He said:
"My Lord: deliver Thou me from the wrongdoing people."
(28:21)

So he watered for them; then he turned away to the shade
and said: "My Lord: I am in need of what Thou hast sent
down to me of good."
(28:24)

He said: "My Lord: help Thou me against the people who
work corruption.")
(29:30)

Those who bear the Throne and those round about it
give glory with the praise of their Lord, and believe in
Him, and ask forgiveness for those who heed warning:
"Our Lord: Thou encompassest all things in mercy and
knowledge, so forgive Thou those who have repented
and followed Thy path, and protect Thou them from the
punishment of Hell!
"Our Lord: make Thou them enter the Gardens of Perpetual
Abode which Thou hast promised them and whoso was
righteous among their fathers, and their wives, and their
progeny — Thou art the Exalted in Might, the Wise —
"And protect Thou them from evil deeds; and he whom
Thou protectest from evil deeds that day, upon him hast
Thou had mercy." And that is the Great Achievement.
(40:7-9)

And We enjoined upon man: towards his parents, good
conduct. His mother bore him with aversion, and brought
him forth with aversion; and the bearing of him and the
weaning of him is thirty months. When he has reached
maturity, and reaches forty years, he says: "My Lord:
direct Thou me to be grateful for Thy favour with which
Thou hast favoured me and my parents, and to work
righteousness pleasing to Thee; and make Thou me
right in my progeny. I have turned to Thee repentant.
And I am of those submitting."
(46:15)

So he called to his Lord: "I am defeated, so help Thou."
(54:10)

And those who came after them, they say: "Our Lord:
forgive Thou us and our brethren who preceded us in
faith, and put Thou not in our hearts rancour towards
those who heed warning. Our Lord: thou art kind and
merciful."
(59:10)

There was for you a good model in Abraham and those
with him when they said to their people: "We are quit
of you and what you serve besides God. We deny you,
and become clear between us and you are enmity and
hatred forever until you believe in God alone," — save the
saying of Abraham to his father: "I will ask forgiveness
for thee, but I have no power for thee against God." —
"Our Lord: in Thee we place our trust; and to Thee have
we turned; and to Thee is the journey's end.
"Our Lord: make Thou not us a means of denial for those
who ignore warning; and forgive Thou us. Our Lord:
thou art the Exalted in Might, the Wise."
(60:4-5)

O you who heed warning: turn to God in sincere repentance. It may be that your Lord will remove from you your evil deeds, and make you enter gardens beneath which rivers flow. The day God will not disgrace the Prophet and those who heed warning with him, their light running before them and on their right hand, they will say: "Our Lord: perfect Thou for us our light, and forgive Thou us; Thou art over all things powerful."

(66:8)

And God has struck a similitude for those who heed warning: — the wife of Pharaoh, when she said: "My Lord: build Thou for me a house with Thee in the Garden, and deliver Thou me from Pharaoh and his deeds, and deliver Thou me from the wrongdoing people."

(66:11)

"My Lord: forgive Thou me and my parents, and him who enters my house as a believer, and the believing men, and the believing women. And increase Thou not the wrongdoers save in ruin!"

(71:28)

OTHER WORKS BY THE AUTHOR

I invite you to read my other books which are available for free at *willyounotreason.com*. Below are the introductions from my two books: "Tyranny 2.0" and "Cosmology of the Qur'an".

Introduction to Tyranny 2.0

We are living under a tyranny disguised as a democracy. The genius of its architects is that they have camouflaged it in the doublespeak of choice, freedom and democracy; but make no mistake, we face a tyranny unparalleled by any of its predecessors in its scale and sophistication. Whereas, the tyrannies of old employed crude methods of torture and mass slaughter to subjugate the masses; Tyranny 2.0 employs the refined scientific method. It applies knowledge gained from the disciplines of biology, chemistry, computer science, mathematics, physics and psychology in its management of the human herd; continuously learning, refining its algorithms and perfecting its methods in order to achieve its ultimate goal of complete control over the human mind.

The fake pandemic of 2020 kicked off the global implementation of totalitarian lockdowns, mandatory face masks and forced injections. This is but a taste of the dystopian future that awaits us if we do not repent, reform and warn. It may sound cliché, but time *is* running out. Tyranny 2.0 is now officially online and our technocratic overlords have made it clear that they mean business.

Yet, even now, most men are unaware (or in denial) that we are living under a tyranny. The truth is that "God guides whom He wills".[1] It is not within my power to *wake* you up, nor can I convince a victim of brainwashing that he, in fact, *is* brainwashed. This book is only for those who understand that we are in the grips of a sophisticated tyranny, and believe in God; for it is God alone who can save us.

The harsh reality is that we are ruled by corrupt, sinful and evil men. It makes no difference whether they call themselves Christians, Jews, Muslims or atheists, nor does it matter whether they are the leaders of the "free world", third-world dictators, directors of intelligence agencies or the Pharaohs of Egypt, these men are workers of corruption and have no qualms about ordering the slaughter of millions to get what they want.

Contrary to popular propaganda, the rulers of our current tyranny are not the champions of the people, but are their very enemies. This is to be expected since the corrupt selection process of Tyranny 2.0 ensures that only the most vile and devious of the lot rise to the top of the power structure.

These evildoers – and their predecessors – have been waging a secret war against mankind for the better part of a century. Their aim is to destroy man's dignity, decency and morality. Ultimately, they wish to extinguish our very soul.

Tyranny 2.0 uses cutting edge *soft* weapons against its principal enemy: men. It uses cellphones, email and social media to track, monitor and surveil us. It leverages the internet and television to deliver devastating payloads of propaganda, pornography and entertainment to keep us docile and apathetic. It markets pharmaceutical weapons of pills, injections and packaged foods to deliver hormone altering chemicals, gene editing instructions and GMO foods to destroy our health. It funds social movements to promote homosexuality, women liberation and racial equality to pervert our cutlture. When all else fails, it deploys drones, smart bombs and mercenaries to kill, slaughter and torture, to obliterate entire nations.

Any reasonable thinking man can now work out that the motive behind such monstrous acts is not "to champion liberty and democracy"[2]

---

1 *The Qur'an*, 28:56.
2 Biden, Joseph R., and Jr. "Why America Must Lead Again." Foreign Affairs, Council on Foreign

across the world. We have been conditioned to accept such outright lies by those in power because this entire system is based on deception.

Tyrants wage war in order to control systems, resources, and people. They know that they must control all resources in order to guarantee their position as the apex predator. However, our enlightened tyrants have come to understand that if they wish to rule forever, they must ultimately control the human mind; and they are tantalizingly close to this goal.

The first rule of any conflict is to know your enemy. All evidence points to the United States – considering its superpower status – as the primary cultural, economic and environmental corrupter in the land, but that is seeing the trees for the forest. The people of the United States – and the Western civilization – have, themselves, been under a continuous assault by a sinister force for the better part of a century. It was only after this force of evil had compromised the religion, culture and family values of the West that it set its sights upon the rest of the world.

What is this sinister force and why is it hell bent on destroying humanity? You may already have a hazy idea of its nature even though modern propaganda has done all that it can to convince you of its non-existence. I am, of course, talking about Satan, the Deceiver. Tyranny 2.0 is based entirely on deception precisely because it is a Satanic tyranny and, as we shall see, deception is *the* modus operandi of Satan.

God in His final revelation to mankind, the Qur'an, warns us of this malevolent being whose objective is nothing short of our utter humiliation and destruction. The seriousness of God's warning cannot be overstated. He exhorts us to take Satan as a clear enemy and exercise our utmost vigilance against his attempts to divert us from the righteous path of God. Satan wishes to enslave us in this world and lead us to Hell in the next; and he achieves this by partnering with tyrants, old and new.

The Qur'an details the account of an ancient tyrant, Pharaoh, who was also in the thrall of Satan. His tyranny used religion, sorcery and finance to subjugate its population; not unlike Tyranny 2.0 which uses science, the entertainment industry and banks to subjugate us. Pharaoh's

Relations, 30 Nov. 2020, www.foreignaffairs.com/articles/united-states/2020-01-23/why-america-must-lead-again.

tyranny committed genocide by slaughtering a certain faction of the population; not unlike Tyranny 2.0 which commits global genocide – the depopulation agenda – by the scientific means of feeding the populace processed GMO foods and pesticide tainted crops, facilitating abortion and, more recently, COVID-19 "vaccines". Pharaoh sought to discover the God of Moses and the means of the heavens; not unlike Tyranny 2.0 which is launching sophisticated telescopes and satellites to peer into the heavens, and constructing state-of-the-art particle accelerators to study the building blocks of the universe.

But, perhaps, the most striking of all connections between Pharaoh's tyranny and Tyranny 2.0 is their use of obelisks to mark their domain. These obelisks are now erected in most of the cities around the world. The most famous of them, the Washington Monument, is a popular tourist attraction in Washington D.C. Every President of the United States faces this obelisk during his swearing in ceremony, promising to protect and defend Tyranny 2.0.

Satan uses the elites of Tyranny 2.0 to implement his agenda of enslaving mankind; and they are rewarded well for their services. However, theirs is a losing deal because on the Day of Judgment, Satan and his followers will enter Hell and remain there forever; an evil end for evil works. If that was the end of the matter, I would not be writing this book. But, unfortunately, it is not.

The people – by informed consent and active participation in this Satanic system – are guilty as well. They worship the idols of Tyranny 2.0 instead of worshipping God. They turn to the idols of state, religion and medicine to seek safety, guidance and health, when they should be seeking these blessings from God. They worship themselves when they should be worshipping God. They fear men when they should be fearing God. These tendencies are termed as *making partners with God* within the theology of the Qur'an, the only unforgivable sin.[3] If the people do not repent and reform, they will enter Hell along with their leaders.

This is a spiritual war and at stake is our very soul. The pain, suffering and humiliation that we experience in this life is but a shadow of the eternal pain and suffering that awaits the apathetic, amoral, and appetite driven souls in Hell.

The Qur'an calls those who believe in God and the life to come to

---

3 The Qur'an 4:48.

work on disciplining and purifying themselves. They must stop consuming the filth churned out by Tyranny 2.0 and struggle to escape, as much as possible, from its grip. God promises His help, provision and refuge to those who resist Satan and assures them a place in the eternal Garden in the Hereafter. We must warn men of the impending judgment of God which will can only be averted from those who fear God and take the Almighty as their sole Ally and Protector.

***

Many of the ideas presented in this book are from the ground-breaking work of Sam Gerrans titled *The Qur'an: A Complete Revelation*. I encourage you to download his work – which is available for free[4] – and go through it carefully.

I would be remiss if I did not mention the impact Alan Watt's talks[5] – have had on my world-view. His piercing insights into the inner workings of this Satanic system and the staggering scale of its deception have influenced many of my own ideas in this work.

All translations, unless otherwise noted, are my own. I have striven to render the Arabic in a literal, direct and consistent manner, being particularly influenced by the unique styles of John J. Arberry, Sahih International and Sam Gerrans. Where a literal translation of a phrase was too confusing, I have opted for a somewhat looser rendering, but have footnoted the literal translation for the interested reader.

Introduction to Cosmology of the Qur'an

In this work, I present the cosmology and astronomy of the Qur'an. Try as you might, you cannot escape the fact that what the Qur'an presents a model of celestial and terrestrial phenomena is utterly irreconcilable with science and the claims of its priesthood – the scientific class. Scientists would have us believe that the universe is an ever expanding, never ending space without any physical boundaries. In this space, countless objects spin, collide and orbit. Utter chaos reigns supreme. The earth is relegated to the status of just another planet among countless others in this limitless universe. The sun is at the center of our solar system

---

4 https://quranite.com
5 http://cuttingthroughthematrix.com

around which all planets – including the earth – revolve.

However, this is not what the Qur'an presents as fact.

The Qur'an repeatedly refers to the sky as a raised physical structure and the ground as a plane. It speaks of seven skies stacked on top of each other. It states that the ground is firmly fixed by mountains and that it is sun and the moon that are in motion, not the ground. However, the lamentable state of affairs is such that Muslims – who vehemently proclaim the Qur'an to be right and true – are unwilling to challenge the false claims presented by science. Even a cursory understanding of the word of God lays bare the lies present in the heliocentric model - to speak nothing of a myriad of other falsehoods peddled by Darwin, Newton and Einstein. If you are uncomfortable with this statement, then I suggest you ponder on what your eyes bear witness to every day: the sun has been travelling across the sky your whole life! You have been blinded by deceivers who would rather you shut out your eyes to the truth. Only a man conditioned by years of propaganda, disinformation and lies10 rejects the testimony of his eyes and claims that it is not the sun that is moving but the very ground itself!

In this work, I will go over the treatment of the words samā and arḍ – and auxiliaries – in the Qur'an. Below are two verses containing these words so we are clear on what is being discussed:

> He who appointed the arḍ a floor and the samā a con-
> struction and sent down from the samā water so He
> brought forth fruits from it for your provision. So do
> not appoint equals to God when you know.
>
> (2:22)

> Or like a cloudburst from samā – in it is darkness, thunder
> and lightning – they put their fingers in their ears against
> the thunder fearing death. And God encompasses the
> unbelievers
>
> (2:19)

The Qur'an uses the word arḍ to denote the ground on which we stand. This word is usually translated as: earth, world or land. I like the rendering of arḍ as ground since this word does not come with baggage.

What I mean by that is that words such as earth and world have been associated with a false spinning globe for so long that it is impossible to get the reader to visualize anything different when reading them. Arḍ is defined in Arabic dictionaries as: earth (as apposed to heaven or as a planet), globe, world, soil, ground, country and land. The Qur'an uses the word samā to denote the sky. This word is usually translated as: sky, heaven or firmament. I keep it simple by rendering it as sky throughout my work. Samā is defined in Arabic dictionaries as: to be high, elevated, raised, erect, lofty, tall, eminent and prominent.

We will investigate various verses in the Qur'an to build a true understanding of the phenomena around us. No trickery or falsehood is employed – personally, I am sick of both. A word on translation: It is understood that all translators have some bias; man is incapable of being truly impartial, try as he may. I am no exception. I have tried my best to render my translation in a direct, literal and consistent manner. I have also consulted a large number of translations and other works in my rendering of Qur'anic verses, a full list of which can be found in the References section. I sincerely advise you to ponder on the information below and not dismiss out of hand that which challenges your knowledge and assumptions. A book claiming to be from God deserves sincere, measured and careful study. May God guide you to His straight path.

Let us begin, then, in the name of God.

REFERENCE

Books

The Qur'an: A Complete Revelation, Sam Gerrans.
The Meaning of the Holy Qur'an, Abdullah Yusuf Ali.
The Holy Bible, King James Version.

Online Resources

corpus.quran.com
reader.quranite.com
quranix.org
studyquran.co.uk

Website

willyounotreason.com